D1319440

THE SOURCE

THE SOURCE
Inspirational ideas for the home

Michael Freeman

eightbooks

CONTENTS

INTRODUCTION

For more than a decade, I have been photographing a range of contemporary houses around the world. What they have in common is the following: they have all had intense thought and effort put into designing their various functions, they are all imaginative, idiosyncratic, and they all appealed to me in one way or another. What they do not share, however, is the usual dead hand of the regular commercial interior designer. Instead, they are all the products of a deep interest in ways of living.

Spreading the net wide, across different cultures, was extraordinarily valuable for me, and ultimately provided the inspiration for this book. Globalization is happening not just in economy, but in ideas about ways of organizing the space in which we live. Drawing on our own cultural traditions is, of course, normal, useful and necessary, but this is a changing world, and it pays to draw inspiration from other sources.

East Asia, particularly Japan, has for the last two decades been an especially fertile source, and not simply because the cultural backgrounds have been so different from Western ones. The trigger for making the region relevant and exciting was the aftermath of the

economic downturn at the end of the eighties. Up to that point, Japan had enjoyed a steady and apparently unstoppable boom that had begun in the sixties. The heady years of insane land prices and increasing wealth did few favours for design, as many clients looked for Western style or something that seemed to better it. Japan led the way for Asia in developing chaotic and ugly urban environments. Yet when the recession hit in 1990, it created conditions for a revival of thoughtful design and architecture. This was by no means universal, but at its best generated designs for living spaces that are at once contemporary, yet draw on traditional principles. One of these principles is flexibility of space, using light methods of division to alter the space plan of a house in an instant. A bedroom can open up into a living area by sliding back wooden or wood-and-paper screen doors and by packing away the futon. Another is the interpenetration of interior and exterior to draw a garden inwards and to project a living space outwards. This, indeed, goes back to older Chinese principles. These are just two concepts among several that run contrary to Western tradition, and yet which are entirely applicable to modern living.

   Until quite recently, design in all forms originating outside the loosely termed "West" was generally thought of as "ethnic", which meant in some vague way locked into a historical tradition, long-established and handed down, resistant to new influences. Furniture and objects sourced in countries such as India or Thailand were predictable and somewhat exotic, usually classifiable as crafts, meaning supposedly made in a village with arcane tools, although more likely mass-produced with poorly paid labour to look like a true craft. It seemed to take a long time for retail outlets in the West and for publishers dealing

with this kind of subject to acknowledge that there were contemporary designers everywhere who were as interested in the modern as they were. Now, as the balance of economy and influence is shifting globally, this kind of myopia seems in the process of being cured. What we now have in the world of design and architecture is a growing cross-fertilisation, and while this happens professionally, I hope this book will go a small way to help broaden it.

The sheer variety of solutions to essentially similar issues of organizing, dividing, and connecting living space motivated this unusual structure. More typically, a book on this subject takes the subject home by home, the unified concept of one designer, architect or house owner. Here, it seemed much more useful to dissect and separate the ideas according to a kind of universal purpose. If we parse living space in general, it falls into the divisions we've used here — the spaces, in turn divided by purpose, the ways of connecting them, of dividing them, and utilities. While there's nothing specially radical in this, it does show the relationships between design ideas and, more important, it is an encouragement to look at homes in terms of their elements, with a view to considering them more carefully. Connection and division in particular tend to fall outside the usual way that home owners have of seeing interiors. A corridor, for example, is clearly a way of connecting rooms within a house, but it is by no means the only way. If you were making a conversion, it might help to go back to the basics of purpose in order to find a different solution.

Related to this lateral way of looking at homes, I've made a deliberate effort to range in scale between micro and macro. In the many homes

RIGHT: Simple forms abound in this spacious double-height reception area. A staircase flows through the room to the right and the external view is reflected in the striking hanging glass dividing wall.

featured here, the photographs take us on a journey in which at times we stand back to see how it all works, and at times we inspect closely, even down to hinges and door handles, to see how these contribute to the whole. The purpose is to rethink. I hesitate to use the word improve, because "home improvement" has become such a cliché as to have lost any sense, but tailoring home space to individual taste and need is certainly the goal. Every single image in this book shows a result that was designed specifically to suit the owner of the space. None of it just happened, or was made anonymously somewhere and just handed over. The sort of interior design commissioned by developers for later sale to who-knows-what client is about the worst thing I can imagine happening in the creation of a house or apartment. If the money is available to design, at least it deserves to be spent thoughtfully. And if not, then there are other ways. As example after example here show, expense is not what ties together the ideas in this book. Many have the elegance of simplicity and thrift, not a bad principle to follow during a period of economic downturn. A number of architects and designers here have explored the desirable features of cheap materials that would be dismissed by less imaginative people — materials such as compressed board, cardboard, rough construction bamboo, tin, and mud plaster.

As a source book of ideas, this is ultimately about the way we choose to live — at least when we can exercise that choice and have the opportunity to do something about our homes, to create them or adjust them to suit our needs. My own interest in architecture and design is not in its formal aspects, but in how it affects living. In one of the most influential essays on architecture, "Building Dwelling Thinking", the

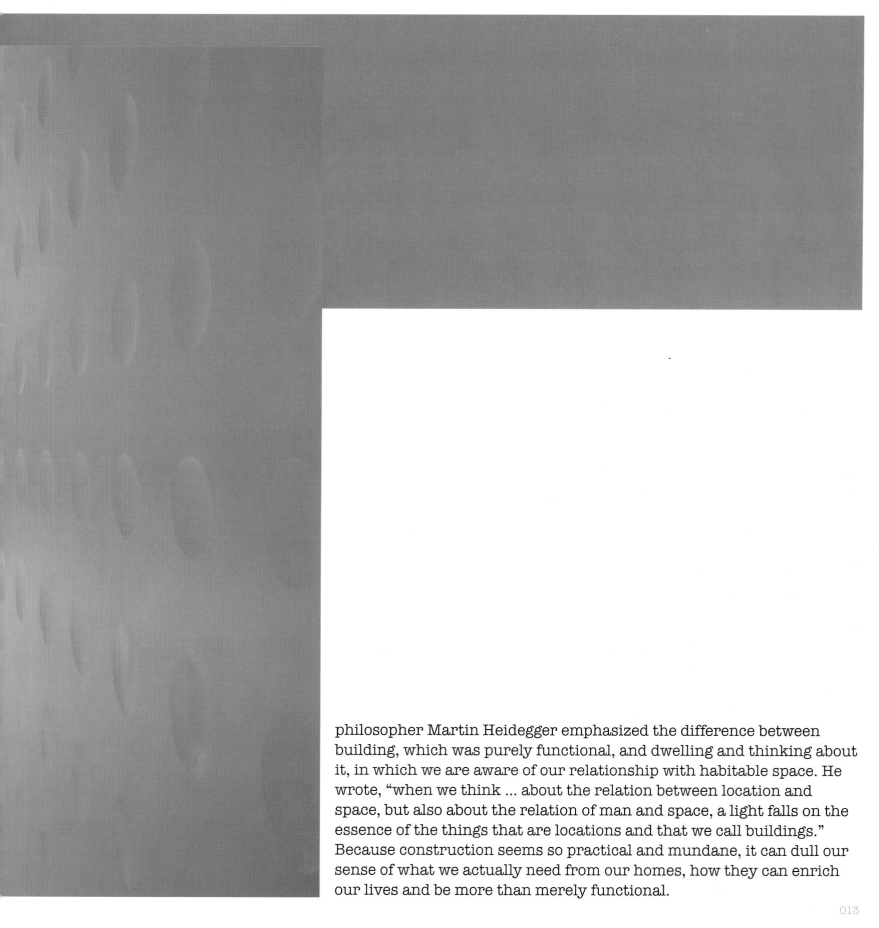

philosopher Martin Heidegger emphasized the difference between building, which was purely functional, and dwelling and thinking about it, in which we are aware of our relationship with habitable space. He wrote, "when we think ... about the relation between location and space, but also about the relation of man and space, a light falls on the essence of the things that are locations and that we call buildings." Because construction seems so practical and mundane, it can dull our sense of what we actually need from our homes, how they can enrich our lives and be more than merely functional.

CONNECT

ENTRANCES
DOORWAYS
STEPS
HALLWAYS
STAIRCASES
CORRIDORS
FLOORS

In the traditional — I might even say conservative — way of thinking about layout, the main functional spaces of a house (living, dining, sleeping) are at the core, and the area given over to entering them and joining them is secondary.

Hence, the traditional Western small house has often featured corridors and stairwells no wider than they need to be, spaces intended to be moved through quickly without spending time, or indeed money. And yet, as we can see here, there are various solutions and strategies, not all of which involve tucking them away conveniently.

But then, it is by no means traditional to group together these transit areas with entrances, as we have done here. Thinking about them as the connections between the primary spaces can be an aid to rethinking their design. For example, they can be made to perform some additional functions, as in some of the entrances with which the chapter begins. It may seem logical to be direct with an entrance and its doorway — simply that here is the house and this is the obvious way to gain access. But some Chinese and Japanese principles suggest a more oblique approach, such as involving a reveal, whether slow or sudden. The approach could meander, or turn a right angle at the last moment. And the entrance itself offers the possibility of being a statement, of having a distinct character that sets the tone for the journey inside.

Corridors typically run around larger spaces, but in some of these designs the architect has chosen to give them presence, mini-spaces in their own right in which their basic form suggests making use of depth of view and perspective. Just inside the main entrance, of course, they can become hallways, where the visitor first experiences the house; in terms of size, even modest hallways can have presence.

If corridors and hallways are the horizontal connectors for a dwelling, staircases and flights of steps are their vertical equivalent.

Indeed, their verticality draws visual attention as long as they are not hidden away between walls, and in the striking variety shown here they are treated in some instances minimally and quietly, in others flamboyantly. One architect chose to hide a stairwell to make it a secret part of the house, while another made it the armature for the entire house, twisting and turning in a display of unexpected angles, materials, and colours.

And finally, the floor. Viewed as a surface over which to move rather than just a necessary boundary to a room, materials and treatments become interesting. Wood, metal, stone, concrete, tiles, even straw can be worked and handled in an infinite number of ways. And, as recurs throughout this book, some of the most interesting are the least expensive, relying on imagination rather than costly materials.

CONNECTENTRANCES

LEFT: The entrance to an extremely narrow building squeezed between two existing blocks in central Tokyo. The offset path and full-length glass help to avoid a sense of constriction.

BELOW AND BELOW RIGHT: A contemporary garden entrance in Shanghai, designed by Sakae Miura, combines a diagonally-set path lined with bamboo and bordered with pebbles. Both the inner door (left) and the outer street door, both sliding, are perforated. The steel blocks on the street (right) contain an opening mechanism — a palm-operated security pad is hidden in the V-shaped aperture.

RIGHT ABOVE: In an extremely narrow house, 130 feet high but tapering from 13 feet to 8 feet, an even narrower interior garden carries a stepping-stone walkway to an open, yet private, bathroom.

FAR RIGHT: Stands of black bamboo line a raised wooden walkway that turns 90 degrees at the end. Just in front of the door (to the right of the picture) is a miniature garden of two mounds of moss on white gravel.

PREVIOUS PAGES:
LEFT: At a beach house north of Mumbai, India, the entrance walkway is a concrete tunnel, entered from one side. Large porthole-like windows are a recurrent theme, this one backlit as an entrance light.

RIGHT: Combining old and new, the entrance to a Japanese-style room has traditional stepping stones, but through a concrete entrance with visible formwork, at the Niki Club, Nasu, Japan.

PAGE LEFT

LEFT: For a house in Tokyo designed by Michimasa Kawaguchi with a theme of dark, subdued quietness, the entrance is intentionally secretive and constricted, leading to a double-height wood door stained black with ink.

RIGHT: In the conversion of a double-bayed 1930s lane house in Shanghai, by architects sciskewcollaborative, both front and back entrances have been reworked to combine wooden and mosaic pathways that interlock and feature curving slopes and cutaways.

ABOVE: From the street door at the end, a concrete pathway set with pebbles leads past a bamboo and wooden wall to the house entrance at right.

LEFT: In a Tokyo house featuring tactile materials (concrete, timber, earthen plaster, and hand-made paper), the entrance path curves around a tiny strip garden, recently planted with maple. The door and all timber surfaces are stained with calligraphy ink.

CONNECTDOORWAYS

FAR LEFT: Timber slatting gives the façade of this London mews house designed by Ian Chee cohesion, and reduces the normal prominence of the door.

FAR LEFT TOP: The view from the stairs.

LEFT: In a conversion of an old warehouse on Suzhou Creek, Shanghai, dating from the 1920s, architect Deng Kun Yan chose to retain the original steel doors, and having cleaned them left them untreated.

BELOW: A simple open metal grille keeps this doorway unobtrusive, allowing the bamboo planting to dominate the façade.

RIGHT: The Art Deco entrance to the Dolores del Rio House in Santa Monica, designed in 1931 by Cedric Gibbons.

BELOW LEFT: Mirror-faced doors on the inside of the entrance to a modernized Shanghai lane house.

BELOW RIGHT: Virginia creeper has been allowed to cover the adobe earth wall surrounding this courtyard house in Santa Fe, for a soft and colourful entrance.

LEFT CLOCKWISE FROM TOP LEFT:
A simple sliding door in white wood contrasts with the black timber façade of this Japanese house.
Two species of bamboo soften this grey and white entrance.
Galvanized aluminium cladding is used for all the exterior surfaces of this Tokyo house, and the semi-industrial style is continued with the aluminium door with porthole window.
A wooden door with an open grid, flanked by a Japanese summer wax tree.
Thin slivers of glass either side of a dark wooden door are a clever device to allow light in at the same time as ensuring privacy.
A sliding wooden door reveals a succession of views back to a small courtyard garden.

TOP LEFT: Suspended staircases are a feature of this villa close to Delhi by Pradeep Pathak, adding to the effect of multi-level connectedness.

FAR LEFT: Here, the architect of this house conversion has made a feature of the steps by fitting them with backlit glass risers.

ABOVE: For minimalist effect, all surfaces except one wooden wall are in glossy white.

LEFT: A steep set of metal steps is used here within the limited space of this entrance to a bedroom.

CONNECTSTEPS

ABOVE: Rough-hewn timber, used for both the triangular slab-like bottom step and an unusual shallow slope to replace conventional steps.

TOP RIGHT: Projecting stone slabs provide a minimal stairway to the roof terrace in this house in Ahmedabad, India, designed by Aniket Bhagwat.

RIGHT: Recycled timber planking used as steps down to the garden in John Hardy's house near Ubud, Bali.

BELOW: For a careful restoration of a 1920s French Concession villa in Shanghai, designer Kenneth Grant Jenkins commissioned a hand-painted de Gournay wallpaper covering.

RIGHT: The main entrance to Frank Lloyd Wright's 1917 Hollyhock House in Los Angeles echoes the stepped and slightly canted construction that gives it a monumental aspect.

CONNECT HALLWAYS

LEFT: The entrance to Norisada Maeda's unusually pillow-shaped Borzoi House cuts into the curve of the building and is directly visible from the bedroom.

RIGHT ABOVE: Square concrete slabs set in black pebbles make a stepping-stone entrance, designed by Michimasa Kawaguchi.

RIGHT BELOW: In the same house as featured above, the main hallway is given presence by positioning the artwork high on the cream walls.

FAR RIGHT: Converted from an old industrial warehouse, the studio of Taiwanese architect Deng Kun Yan features a variety of textures. In the approach to the huge sliding door, a circular window cut to the side recalls traditional Chinese moon-gates.

CONNECTSTAIRCASES

ABOVE: A staircase of wooden steps rising on a
single inclined steel girder.

PREVIOUS PAGES: When Pete Oetken converted this four-storey house into eight different floor levels front and back, the staircase was created on site, flowing organically around the different levels and rooms.

RIGHT: Steps in expanded steel lathing set in steel troughs, topped with toughened glass sheets.

BELOW: Minimal supports for these black-painted wooden steps are white plastic-coated steel rods hanging from the ceiling.

RIGHT: A single zig-zag cutout in brushed steel.

ABOVE: Steps hug the side of this double-height room, leading to a timber balcony that runs around two of the walls.

RIGHT: Reciprocating stairs in highly finished painted metal and wood are sandwiched between raw concrete with light spilling through the translucent glass brick wall behind.

FAR RIGHT: The steep, ladder-like pitch of these steps not only saves space, but also helps to isolate the upstairs studio from the living area below.

LEFT: Modern interventions in the form of a utilitarian hanging light and commercial vehicle-style mirrors add to this elegantly finished London staircase.

BELOW: Wedge-shaped wooden steps project directly from the wall, without extra support.

BELOW LEFT: Similar to the construction on page 36, this wooden staircase rises on a single, centrally placed timber beam.

ABOVE: Both staircase and walls are all in brushed steel, with concealed strip-lighting defining the right edge as it ascends to the dark upper floor.

FAR LEFT: Steps and walls plastered in a cream-coloured roughened texture using a terrazzo technique for a seamless effect. The progressive lightening from the light well where the steps turn above helps to expand the space perceptually.

LEFT: Concealed lighting of a different kind is here achieved by placing it behind a false wall of pine shaved with a hand-axe.

LEFT: White-painted steps make a subtle contrast with the wooden wall on one side and its warm reflection in the polished white wall opposite.

FAR LEFT: An intentionally secretive narrow stairway, its steps clad in slate and walls in polished concrete.

BELOW: Access to this contemporary version of a Japanese *tatami* room is from the upper floor via a steel staircase with wooden steps and no risers.

ABOVE: A single spiral staircase in white-painted steel, with fan-shaped treads and a tubular guardrail, rises through all three floors of this narrow property.

LEFT: A light, open metalwork staircase leads down to the tiled court with a shallow pool from an upper bridge that connects to the house.

RIGHT: Steel plates projecting from the wall of this spacious double-height reception area carry a staircase that flows with the curve of the wall.

ABOVE: Sandblasted glass steps lit from below by concealed low-wattage tungsten lamps.

TOP RIGHT: The staircase in this Shanghai film and television production company contributes to the industrial design ethic, in blue-painted steel with toughened glass treads.

RIGHT: A wide staircase in steel and green glass, occupying a three-storey well, is lit from both above and below, and forms a major feature of this villa interior.

ABOVE LEFT: For the lower part of this staircase, a simple, flat steel frame supports one edge of the wooden steps that project from the wall.

FAR LEFT: A plain tubular steel guardrail protects this low-profile staircase fitted to one wall of a double-height lobby area with pond.

LEFT: In the conversion of a Shanghai lane house by Peter Oetken, the lower section of the staircase is finished in red Biazza mosaics.

ABOVE: A sliding steel staircase suspended between two tracks, one recessed into the concrete ceiling, the other in the wooden floor, slides out for access to the upper floor, but fits flush with the cupboards when not needed.

RIGHT: The handrail for this narrow staircase is sculpted into the white wall, both for minimalist effect and to save space.

CONNECTCORRIDORS

LEFT: A heavy internal wall of unfinished concrete is opened up by a striking circular hole, bisected by a diagonal beam that supports the adjacent staircase.

BELOW: Bamboo poles on the other side of a glass door create a textured effect and match the colour of the corridor walls.

049

051

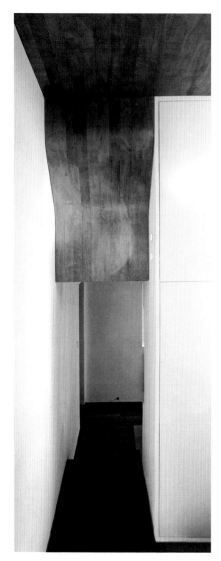

ABOVE: An undulating wooden ceiling mirrors the floor and steps.

RIGHT: A first-floor connecting corridor with reinforced glass floor and glass walls.

FAR RIGHT: A semicircular entrance vestibule with niche continues with a concrete corridor, all finished in a roughened hand-chipped style known as *hatsuri* in Japan.

PAGE RIGHT CLOCKWISE FROM TOP LEFT:
A space-saving floor hatch in the corridor of this exceptionally narrow house.
The false drop ceiling, with recessed lighting, is a clever device for making the corridor appear longer than it actually is.
A hollow circular tower over the corridor functions as a light well.
An entrance corridor lined with louvred glass panels.

PREVIOUS PAGES:

LEFT: The combination of polished concrete with the formworks still showing, and sandblasted glass, creates a surprising unity for this entrance lobby.

MIDDLE: Plain polished white for all surfaces enhances the glow of daylight at the end of this semi-basement corridor.

RIGHT: A sophisticated use of lighting, which includes uplighting through a glass floor, gives a striking shadowless and weightless feeling to this upper-floor corridor.

DIVIDEFLOORS

LEFT: *Kawara* are traditional Japanese clay roofing tiles, used here as patterned flooring by architect Kan Izue. Most are inserted end-on into tightly-packed gravel.

ABOVE: Dark grey sea pebbles are randomly inlaid into a concrete floor to create a contrast with the white stones surrounding a circular bed of shrubs.

ABOVE: An undulating floor of granite blocks cut to different heights animates the entrance to a modern Japanese tea ceremony room.

ABOVE RIGHT: Pebbles and small pieces of coloured ceramic and glass set into the concrete entrance to a house.

RIGHT TOP: A simpler and less rigorous pattern of Japanese *kawara* tiles than the arrangement on the previous pages.

RIGHT: Industrial non-slip aluminium plate used to vary the texture of flooring in a living room.

FAR RIGHT: A polished stone floor extends the depth of this lobby by reflection.

ABOVE: Pale natural wood used by architect Chitoshi Kihara matches the forest setting of a weekend retreat near Kyoto, Japan.

LEFT: Dark polished wood was chosen for this intentionally dimly-lit basement study to give the room weight and presence.

FAR LEFT: Rough-hewn planks, their gaps and cracks filled with white plaster, cut strongly through a more conventional wooden floor in the house of architectural historian Terunobu Fujimori in Japan.

FROM LEFT: Small mirrored glass square set irregularly in earthen tiles; old Chinese bricks re-used as flooring in a Chiang Mai hotel; marble tiles in a geometric pattern; fragments of malachite.

FROM LEFT: Old railway ties cut and laid end-on to their grain; Japanese *tatami* mats laid non-traditionally without cloth edging; tropical hardwood planking connected with a butterfly joint.

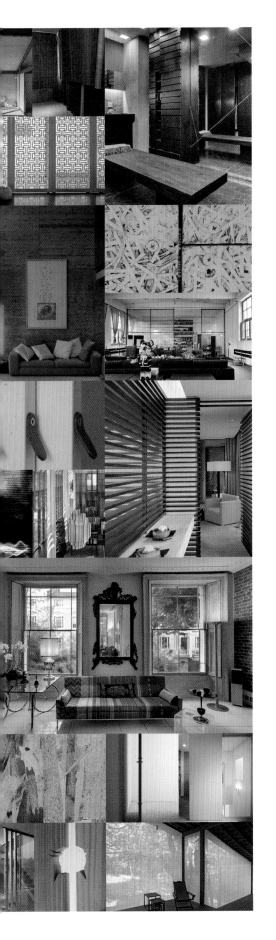

DIVIDE

WALLS

PARTITIONS

SCREENS

DISPLAYS

DOORS

HANDLES

WINDOWS

BLINDS

CURTAINS

CEILINGS

What connects, divides. This essential ambiguity in living spaces is more easily accepted and understood in Chinese and Japanese tradition than in the West. Screens, windows, partitions, and even curtains and blinds, indeed close off and separate, but they also open spaces to each other, either physically or just visually.

This dual functionality is further enhanced by a particular Asian principle that we will look at in more detail in the next chapter — the interpenetration of interior and exterior. Key to this concept is a deliberate lack of definition between the limits of the house and the courtyard or garden which adjoins it. In this chapter, however, we stress the separating function of a wide range of materials.

Because of the many subtle differences among dividers, we have broken down the elements into walls, partitions, screens, blinds, curtains, as well as the seemingly more distinct doors and windows. Within these sub-groups, you will see examples that could plausibly have been in one or two of the others, such as windows that roll back to open the house to the terrace and curtains that replace walls. Not surprisingly, this ambiguity has encouraged, in the contemporary examples shown here, experimentation with an especially wide variety of materials, and particularly in the range between transparent and translucent.

Partitions and screens reflect another Asian living concept, lightness and flexibility, which in turn affect the use of space by making it easy to open and close sections. Shown here are a variety of solutions for

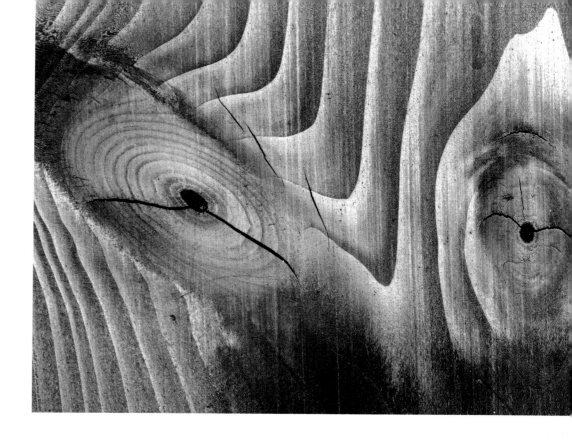

keeping the footprint of these light dividers to an absolute minimum, and concealing them when not in use. The tradition of using paper stretched tightly over a thin wooden frame has been worked on and evolved into glass and plastic. Notable original materials used in other forms of divider are knitted polypropylene shade netting, fine chain-link, corrugated polycarbonate, mud plaster, and blowtorch-burnt wood.

Originality here extends beyond choice of unexpected materials into re-purposing and into new forms and shapes. In one apartment, the owner has hung curtains on walls rather than windows in order to soften the interior, while in a Kyoto house, Jun Tamaki uses a series of white polyester curtains to create changing divisions within a large white cube. In another apartment, the owner-architect has created a complete second skin of curving, organic walls in mud and straw over wire mesh. And as we can see, even collections of art and other objects can themselves form dividers between spaces.

DIVIDEWALLS

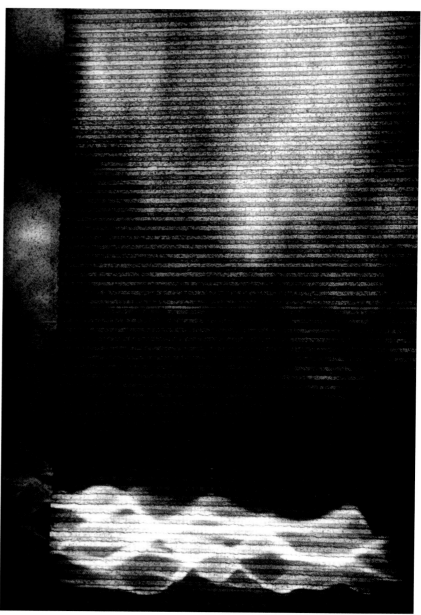

ABOVE: Ceiling spotlights aimed down towards a shallow pool create shifting wavelike reflections that enliven an otherwise austere ribbed concrete wall.

LEFT: Material and textural variety dominates this open living space, combining concrete with exposed formwork, timber, and central divider incorporating fireplace and chimney in stone.

ABOVE: Concrete interior walls roughened by chiselling in the style known as *hatsuri* in a Tokyo house by Michimasa Kawaguchi.

ABOVE LEFT: Raw concrete, the formwork supplied by wooden planking.

LEFT: Hand-cut Chinese granite, fashioned with diagonal joints that recall Peruvian Inca stonework but much thinner, clads the entrance to this Singapore residence.

ABOVE RIGHT: Pressure-opening full-height cupboard doors without handles, covered with veneer curved at the edges, form a simple, natural-looking wall to this dining room.

RIGHT: Designed by Rajiv Saini, this dining room has walls of thin sandstone slabs (the low cost of stone in India makes it a viable option for many surfaces). Repoussé metal floral decorations were applied later.

FAR RIGHT: Original brick in a 1930s Shanghai apartment left exposed in this recent conversion.

ABOVE: The reflective qualities of polished granite flanking the entrance to this Bangkok house designed by the A49 practice make a smooth progression to the glass walls beyond.

ABOVE: Mud and straw fashioned over wire mesh into curved walls create an "earth house" on the top floor of a nondescript Tokyo office block.

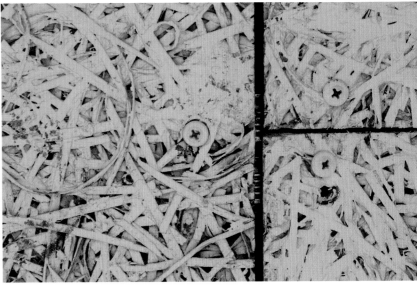

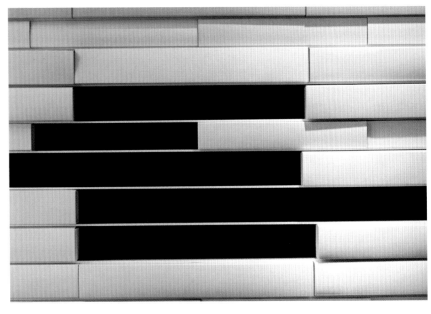

ABOVE: A hand-built interior dry granite wall.

RIGHT FROM TOP: Translucent polycarbonate sheeting riveted to diagonal timber trusses.
Compressed and hardened ribbons of card painted white make lightweight, sound-deadening panels.
Coloured paper strips made into boxes are slotted into ribs to cover this wall in the manner of tiles.

PAGE RIGHT:

TOP LEFT: A black-painted slatted wooden wall surrounds this house by architectural practice A.L.X. like a skin – a kind of curtain wall – making a foil for the all-white traditional Japanese storehouse next door.

RIGHT AND BELOW LEFT: Borrowing a traditional Japanese technique for fire prevention and against rot, architect Jun Tamaki blowtorched cedar planking for the high surrounding wall of this Osaka residence.

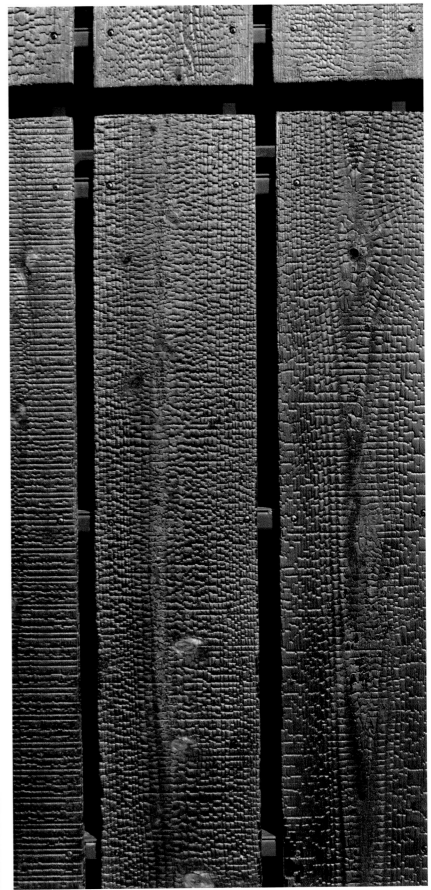

FROM LEFT: Chain-link cladding (left and centre) creates a curtain wall around a tubular shell in a house by Masahide Ikuyama in Takarazuka, Japan; wooden planking stained with diluted black calligraphy ink.

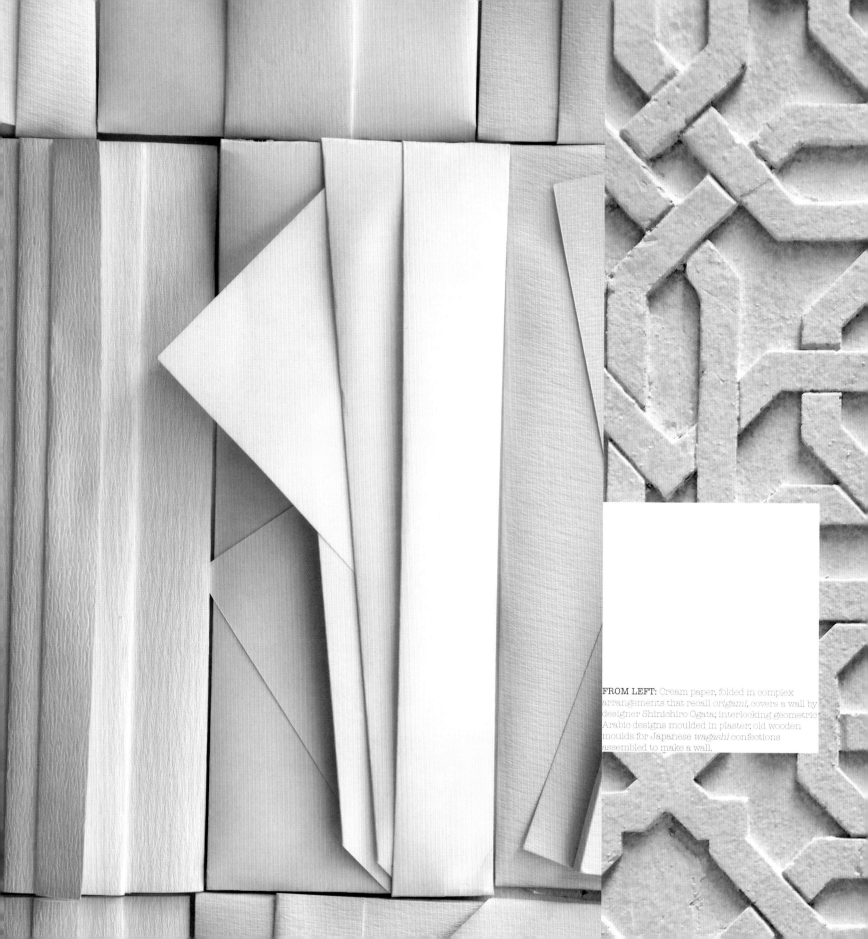

FROM LEFT: Cream paper, folded in complex arrangements that recall *origami*, covers a wall by designer Shinichiro Ogata; interlocking geometric Arabic designs moulded in plaster; old wooden moulds for Japanese *wagashi* confections assembled to make a wall.

FROM LEFT: Hand-chiselled granite cladding; timber planking with joints filled with white plaster; woven bamboo matting; layers of paper individually painted in different shades of red.

DIVIDEPARTITIONS

ABOVE: Glass walls divide and unify at the same time in this apartment by Norisada Maeda. Here, a hexagonal section encloses a light well.

LEFT: Floor-to-ceiling glass walls divide and interact with the sloping ceiling of this polygonal country retreat, designed by Makoto Yamaguchi.

PAGE LEFT:

TOP: Sliding panels covered front and back with stretched paper allow temporary opening and closing of a family study area.

BOTTOM LEFT: Diagonally cut mirrors increase the sense of space in the dressing room of designer JinR's Beijing apartment.

BOTTOM RIGHT: Three sliding wooden panels, here closed up centrally, control access between this room, the landing, and corridor at left and the staircase from ground level at right.

LEFT: Diagonally woven bamboo strips are commonly used in China for concrete formwork, but here they are made into prefabricated structural laminates by architect Shigeru Ban.

BELOW LEFT: Cross beams at the front and rear of this open-plan residence support sliding panels, but these can, as with the nearest beam, be removed completely and stacked in a cupboard.

ABOVE: A tiny apartment retro-fitted by designer Toshihiko Suzuki with water pipes and plumbing fixtures, with the bathroom screened off by corrugated polycarbonate sheeting attached to a curved wall of pipes.

ABOVE: Two low interior walls, stepped and curved, make a semi-partition for a central study area within a living room, and are thick enough to function as counter and shelf space.

LEFT: Wooden free-standing panels partially divide the different functions of this open-plan house for a close-knit small family.

DIVIDESCREENS

ABOVE: Sliding panels on the mezzanine of the Eames house, California, draw on Japanese principles.

LEFT: In a house in Bali designed by Ian Chee, sliding panels are in opalescent glass.

FAR LEFT: A clean modern version of Japanese sliding *shoji* paper screens, without the customary thin wooden slats.

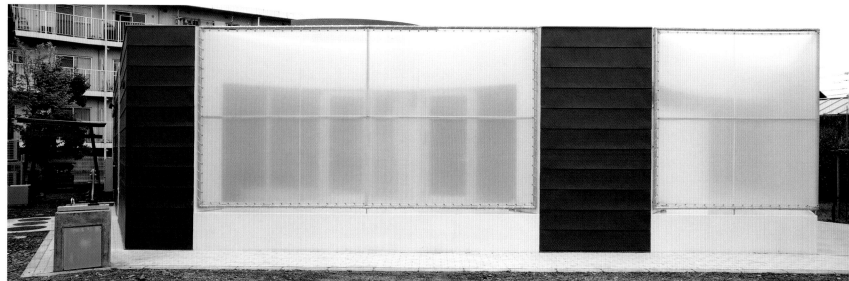

LEFT: White plastic mesh screens held under tensile strength combine light with privacy for this house by architect Norisada Maeda. The house is called "Fontana" in allusion to the the Italian painter famous for his ripped canvases.

ABOVE: Sliding *shqji* paper screens run the length of the living area in this glass-walled house.

RIGHT: For a room within a room, designed by Michimasa Kawaguchi, non-traditional curved paper *shqji* screens were made by a local craftsman.

FROM LEFT: Contemporary patterns of dividing paper screens vary proportion and angle (left and centre); fine metal mesh provides a different kind of screening effect, reducing light while allowing a softened, hazy view through to the terrace from the living room.

ABOVE: To allow air to circulate through this architect's studio near Mumbai, Bijoy Jain chose a finely-knitted polypropylene mesh made for shade netting used in agriculture.

LEFT: Paper stretched on both sides of a frame makes a more substantial form of sliding screen.

RIGHT:
TOP ROW FROM LEFT: Clear plastic strands extruded by hand forming a web that covers a glass screen.
Backing a wooden board drilled with holes with a separately lit blue-painted surface adds a decorative three-dimensional finish.
The side of a staircase designed by Terunobu Fujimori is opened with fancifully carved outlines of a whiskered cat.

BOTTOM ROW FROM LEFT: Another variation of a paper screen, using thin dividing slats.
Crossed slats fill squares in this wooden screen dividing two halves of a room.
Wooden slats in a metal frame are offset between horizontal layers.

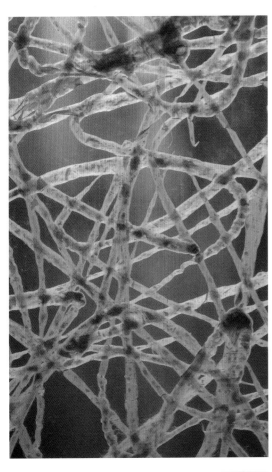

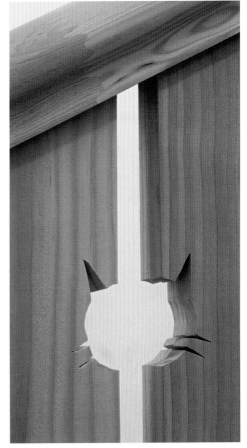
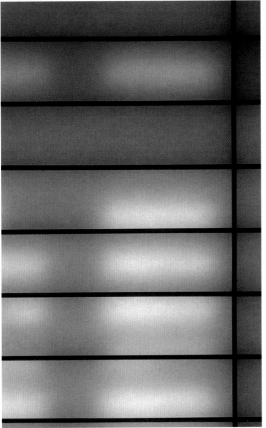

DIVIDEDISPLAYS

ABOVE: Two works by Maarten Baas, a burnt sideboard from his Smoke series, and a stand from his subsequent Clay series, in a London dining room.

LEFT: Simply cut from plywood sheets, a series of Indian-style cusped arches makes display shelving in this Jaipur apartment.

FAR LEFT: In the entrance hall of the residence of Beijing artist Sui Jianguo, a Chinese altar carries a set of the artist's well-known "Mao Suit" ceramics.

LEFT: Concealed strip lighting turns this alcove into a backlit display area.

BELOW: Wooden cupboards in post-modern style by designer Shigeru Uchida house a ceramic collection, and have a central window to display a single piece even when closed.

BOTTOM: In a Mumbai apartment by Rajiv Saini, a white marble Jain statue against a vermilion backdrop separates the two areas of white display shelving.

ABOVE: A Japanese sweetshop designed by Shinichiro Ogata, with walls constructed of wooden boxes (left) and origami-folded paper (right).

LEFT: Downlighting and a translucent shelf lit from below define a display alcove designed by Edward Suzuki.

FAR LEFT: Recessed alcoves with painted interiors, by Rajiv Saini.

DIVIDEDOORS

LEFT: A pivoting door between this basement kitchen and the small terrace outside.

FAR LEFT: A set of wood-framed glass doors both pivot and slide on channels in the floor and ceiling allowing an uninterrupted view of the sea beyond the wood decking.

BELOW: The pivoting point of this wooden door is set in from the wall, so that when open it appears to be light and free-standing.

ABOVE: An adaptation of the traditional Chinese moon gate makes a bedroom door in the Pudong apartment of Zhong Yaling, designed by the owner.

LEFT: The traditional Japanese *shoji* – a sliding screen with *washi* paper stretched over the wooden frame – has many applications in contemporary dwellings, in saving space and adding lightness.

ABOVE: Chinese characters carved into a heavy wooden door are juxtaposed by brushed metallic reveals.

LEFT: Horizontal wooden slats attached to the door and walls provide a continuity of surface in this Taiwanese house.

ABOVE: A metal door with porthole follows the industrial design look of a film production company's offices.

RIGHT: Oversized welded brass keys form the two ventails of a door in this Delhi apartment.

105

DIVIDEHANDLES

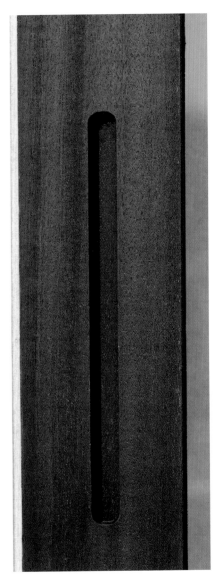

ABOVE FROM LEFT: For a sliding Japanese *shqji* screen, with stretched paper, a small wooden panel with circular finger hole.
A doorknob by Ian Chee, in the shape of a beach pebble, cast in polished metal.
Metal tabs, each recessed into the ends of a pair of sliding cupboard doors.
Also for a sliding door, a long recessed groove is designed for several fingers at once.

FAR LEFT: A thin, curving polished steel handle works well against opaque glass doors.

LEFT: Leather tags screwed into the end of a set of sliding doors.

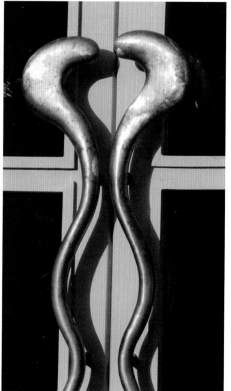

CLOCKWISE FROM TOP LEFT: A tree branch with minimal work done to it makes a pleasing rustic door handle.
An Art Deco handle in red glass and steel, set in a modern glass door.
A found branch is used for this delightful outside toilet in the woods surrounding a Finnish country house.
Modern Indian handles in the form of two inward-facing *nagas* – mythical serpents.
Hand-finished brass for a pair of old Indian repoussé doors.

FAR LEFT: Here, the handle is part of a custom-built entrance in perforated steel plate.

DIVIDEWINDOWS

LEFT: A modern take on a classic Georgian house in Primrose Hill, London. Here the original wooden shutters for the sash windows have been stripped back to reveal the wood beneath.

111

ABOVE: A corner window provides controlled views of the garden from this bedroom and study.

RIGHT: Recessed into the thick wall, these three windows are shaped and sited for their design effect.

ABOVE: A mezzanine bedroom takes advantage of two skylight windows in this house in London.

LEFT: An intimate, semi-concealed study has a skylight window, another facing internally into the house, and a third "floor" window.

TOP LEFT: Converging curved windows open onto a lens-shaped courtyard, one of several in the Fontana House, also featured on page 090.

TOP RIGHT: On the first floor of this house, windows on all sides open onto the interior courtyard.

LEFT: Folding windows open fully to expose the living and kitchen area of this London mews house to the terrace, designed by Ian hee.

ABOVE: An oval-plan timber-framed house designed by Kohei Sato features wrap-around windows with vertical wooden slats.

ABOVE: When open, this curved dining room window projects into the street, blurring the distinction between private and public space.

BELOW: This minimal dwelling exaggerates the lack of any small windows on the street side projection by setting the only interior view within a deep recess.

RIGHT: This Japanese property perched high on a hillside uses louvre windows to both present the view and allow for the placement of objects within each recess.

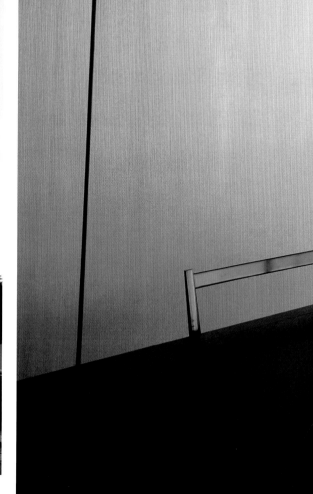

ABOVE AND RIGHT: All in the same house designed by Michimasa Kawaguchi, windows that are cut to reveal specific sections of the view outside, one a thin vertical strip, another horizontal for the study, and a third in the hallway set high in the wall.

BOVE: A small square window in this
athroom is set to give a precisely framed
ew of the minimalist terrace outside.

LEFT: A round window in an Osaka house positioned exactly to look onto a cherry blossom tree that flowers briefly in Spring.

ABOVE: Two porthole windows flanking asymmetrically a large mirror.

TOP LEFT: Translucent fabric stretched over a circular, barred frame.

TOP MIDDLE: A traditional Suzhou Chinese window in carved stone and a geometric pattern.

ABOVE LEFT: Thin sheets of mica, a traditional old form of window in the American Southwest.

ABOVE RIGHT: Coloured glass brings to mind stained glass and spiritual associations.

ABOVE AND RIGHT: Small handmade windows in transparent resin contain embedded open-ended boxes which function as backlit display cases for objects.

ABOVE: Roughly cut round openings in an unusual interior mud wall, covered with wire netting.

DIVIDEBLINDS

ABOVE: Floor-to-ceiling cloth blinds offer selective on-demand privacy for a bedroom and bathroom from the landing.

FT: Three translucent vertical blinds for s all-metal room allow the view to be ntrolled – here restricted to the bamboo ove outside.

ABOVE: In the cubic design of this "9 *Tsubo* House", named for a traditional Japanese area measurement, designed by Makoto Koizumi, each square window is fitted with a sliding tranlsucent glass panel and a sliding paper *shqji* screen for different permutations.

ABOVE: Rustic roll-down bamboo blinds open for a full view of the surrounding forest.

LEFT: Translucent white fabric blinds pull down over the diagonal wooden trusses of this timber house.

ABOVE: Finely linked steel chain curtains divide the mezzanine area from the double-height living room in this house.

DIVIDECURTAINS

LEFT AND BELOW: Kyoto-based architect Jun Tamaki used white polyester curtains as a way for the owner to reconfigure the house space according to mood, from open-plan to enclosed-yet-light.

ABOVE: Restaurant and nightclub owner JinR used white curtains for her apartment bedroom as a simple method of softening an otherwise ordinary space.

RIGHT TOP: Artist Chris Cook painted large paper sheets in subtly different shades of re[?] to create a layered wall covering for this roo[?]

BELOW: Architect Koichi Sakata hung thin white nylon curtains from a circular rail in the centre of the communal living/dining area to allow an instant private dining area.

RIGHT: Long green drapes add a simple, strong colour theme to an otherwise neutra[?] furnished space, and also help to draw in the view of trees outside.

DIVIDECEILINGS

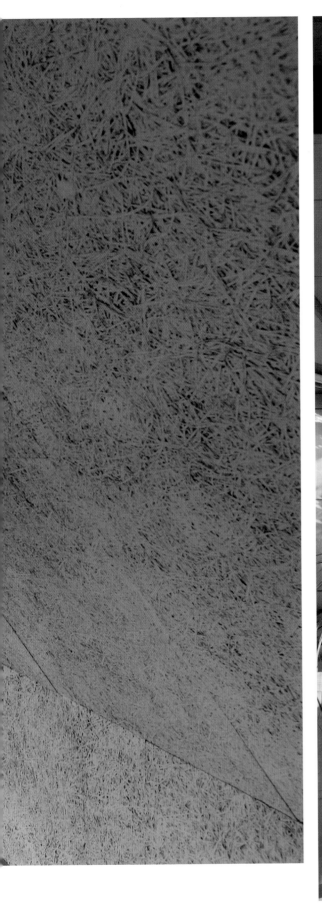

LEFT: Planning regulations in Tokyo regarding light obstruction make diagonal roofs like this common. But architect Toshiaki Ishida chose to make it a feature of the interior, albeit an unusual one, finished in grey cement board.

RIGHT: Exposed and unpainted wood dominates the interior, from floor, walls, and beams, to include the ceiling.

LEFT: Recessed lighting and handmade paper sheets suspended in rows from the ceiling give a soft atmosphere to this dining room.

RIGHT: Plywood panels make an inexpensive and warm method of creating a vaulted ceiling over a living room.

ABOVE: Painted steel beams support an exposed roof of tiles in a modern interpretation of a traditional Thai roof in a house near Pattaya.

RIGHT: Black bamboo fills the spaces between wooden boards and provides additional support on a ceiling.

FAR RIGHT: Rolls of handmade Japanese paper, with tungsten lights above, make an unusual false ceiling.

PAGE RIGHT: Paint-sprayed branches in a Beijing clubhouse basement create an exotic finish to a simple concrete ceiling.

SPACE

LIVING ROOMS
DINING ROOMS
STUDIES
QUIET SPACES
PLAY
LIGHTING
MEZZANINES
BALCONIES
COURTYARDS
INSIDE OUTSIDE
TERRACES
URBAN GARDENS

The two most significant movements in the design of contemporary living space have, on the face of it, been in conflicting directions. One is a move towards open-plan, particularly evident in conversions, whether of small terrace houses or of lofts and semi-industrial properties.

The other is a trend towards new and specialized spaces devoted to just one activity. Both are responses to our changing way of life, particularly in urban and metropolitan areas, and they are not necessarily in opposition, even though one is essentially a blurring of living functions and the other is a sharpening and more precise definition of activities.

The move towards removing divisions and inhabiting a single larger space happens because an increasing number of people are prepared to accept that eating (at least) is not necessarily the formal event it once was, and can take place flexibly in the living space. The clear advantage of doing this is a larger room, and once again, some Asian principles can help — lightweight, quickly moved partitions can make an effective compromise between permanently open and divided. Moreover, living area is increasingly under pressure in cities, with many people having to accept less than they would like because of the cost. Any strategies to increase the sense of space are valuable, and the most straightforward is this.

At the same time, some activities are becoming more concentrated in the home. Notably, there is a general increase in the number of people working from home, especially supported by broadband access. This calls for some allocation of work or study space, even if it has to be shared in time or space. Even without the need for real work, the equipment — computers and their peripherals — are now

standard in any contemporary home. An extension of study space is what we call here "quiet space". This is a kind of meditative space, an area set aside for the individual that excludes the normal rush of activity from the outside. This is still very much a minority idea, but slowly gathering momentum. And third, the nature of entertainment is changing. The piano in the living room is long gone, perhaps sadly, but advances in television, video, and gaming, and the increasing affordability of large screens, make a home theatre an interesting option for a number of people.

The idea of interpenetration of exterior and interior that we saw in the last chapter brings into play a different kind of space — urban gardens, terraces, balconies, and courts. However small these are, and in a city dwelling even a few square feet outside can be a luxury, there are ways of drawing them in to the living experience of the home. Paradoxically, having a small outside space to work with encourages a greater concentration of attention, as some of the small balcony examples that follow demonstrate.

SPACELIVINGROOMS

PREVIOUS PAGES: The tube-like structure of this house, cantilevered out over a hillside above the town of Takarazuka, Japan, allows the living room to project right into the view without any foreground element.

LEFT: Living room of a modern Delhi farm-style house. The circular coffee table in this double-height living room is custom-designed and composed of 12 different timbers. The floor-to-ceiling glass walls look out onto the surrounding estate gardens. The grey sliding screens behind the sofa lead into the dining room beyond.

RIGHT: Double-height living room in glass, marble, and aluminium, using a contemporary minimalist architectural vocabulary, in a large new villa in Pudong, Shanghai, designed by Rocco Yim. The contemporary chandeliers are in twisted resin strips.

ABOVE: Living room in a white-themed Beijing apartment with marble-topped table in four sections and recessed low alcove for the television and books.

LEFT: Living area of a penthouse suite overlooking Suzhou Creek, Shanghai, in white and beige, with white partition curtain separating it from the bedroom.

FT: Living room in a converted Shanghai [ ] e house, with French doors opening onto [ ] garden. The original Art Deco geometry is [ ]phasized with an all-white finish to walls, [ ]r, and ceiling.

LOW FAR LEFT : Living room by Indian [ ]signer Rajiv Saini, featuring a large [ ]corative glass panel painted with images of [ ]ndin, the sacred bull associated with Shiva. [ ] two-section coffee table is in local [ ]dstone, each square carrying a single [ ]ite flower inlay in *pietra dura*.

LOW LEFT: Living room of a modern [ ]dian country retreat on the outskirts of [ ]medabad in Gujarat, India, featuring bright [ ]ours from local fabrics and rugs to give it [ ]ghtness, energy, and a rustic-but-modern [ ]ling.

GHT: A living room in which the seating [ ]ea is screened off by two double-sided [ ]ntings supported in glass sheets. Natural [ ]terials used in the room include rice paper [ ] the walls, linen on the sofas and cane [ ]tting on the ceiling.

LOW: Living room of a a modern Delhi [ ]m-style house. Natural stone finishes [ ]me the painting.

LOW RIGHT: Living area in the restricted [ ]ace of a Hong Kong Mid-Levels apartment, [ ]h wooden bookcase and wooden coffee [ ]le reinterpreting a traditional Chinese [ ]ud pattern motif.

LEFT: Two steps separate the dining and kitchen area from the raised living area in this London mews house conversion. A low glass wall protects the stairwell at left. Folding glass doors concertina to the right to open the entire area to the small roof terrace beyond.

ABOVE: In this top-floor conversion of a large London house, space is saved by constructing a mezzanine bedroom above, allowing a sitting area below.

LEFT: Opening the two large rooms of this London house at the raised entrance level allows one to enter from front and rear through the generous window area. A red Balzac chair with stool by Matthew Hilton separates this living area from the other half (behind the camera).

BELOW: A contrasting mixture of furnishings give individuality to this living area in a terrace conversion in London, including a Dodo chair by Toshiyuki Kita, Meteor low table by Arik Levy, and a traditional Japanese *tansu*.

ABOVE: The living area of the Greenberg House, a 1991 Los Angeles house by the Mexican architect Ricardo Legorreta. Mexican influences are felt in the viga-like ceiling beams, the open access to the garden (out of shot at left), and in the ochre and earth-toned palette that suffuses this room.

RIGHT: The living room of one of the Willow Glen Houses, 1973-1975, Los Angeles, by Peter de Bretteville. The industrial design effect is predicated on an auto body shop, and features white interior surfaces, plastic laminate surfaces, and rubber stud tile floors. A circular-sectioned steel ducting fulfils the role of a chimney breast, over a severely stepped fireplace.

BELOW RIGHT: The double-height living room of the Lovell Beach House by Rudolph Schindler, built in 1925 at Newport Beach, California. Bedrooms and sleeping decks are suspended on the gallery above.

BELOW: In Japanese Post-Modern style, the living room of this house in Nagoya designed by Shigeru Uchida occupies half of the barrel-vaulted main building. A massive wooden wall contains storage units and air ducts. Glass doors at left open onto a courtyard.

ABOVE: The living room of the Bamboo House near the Great Wall north of Beijing, designed by Kengo Kuma and clad with inexpensive bamboo poles, which in bright sunlight create a striking pattern of light and shadow across the room.

RIGHT: In the aptly named House of Shadows, designed by Studio MY, the view down from the balcony of the upper floor onto the living area, which opens through full-height glass doors to the small water garden at right.

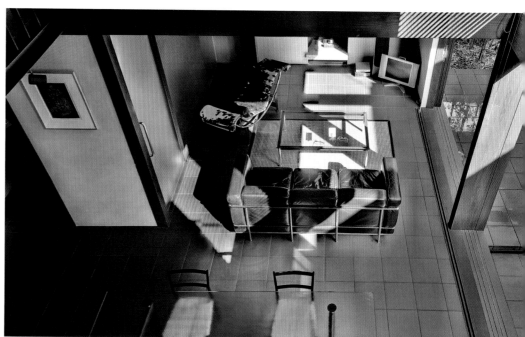

ABOVE: Living room in the house of an art collector on the northern outskirts of Beijing. Designed by neighbouring artist Shao Fan, who also designed the furniture, this is part of a compound of several friends. The house opens south-facing to a courtyard on the left, and a full glass wall allows light to flood into the white-painted interior.

RIGHT: In a house with very limited space, the living area is separated from the staircase by an unobtrusive glass wall to give some extra sense of spaciousness.

FAR RIGHT: The corner of a double-height living room in Pudong, Shanghai, shaded on this north side by grilles of aluminium tubes outside.

FT
OCKWISE FROM TOP: With a panoramic
w of Shanghai's Huangpu River, Zhong
ng's living room combines strongly
oured fabrics with antique rugs and chests.
olished granite floor reflects two striking
ks of art, a pentaptych painting and a
lptured head by Ravinder Reddy.
signer Andrew Norrey finished this
noiserie-themed room with walls in a deep
lacquered crackle glaze, with a black
ing.
e 25 by 45-foot living room of the 1931
ric Gibbons house is in high-Art Deco
le, featuring a polished black terrazzo floor,
lt-in banquettes, concealed uplighting, and
igh, stepped ceiling.

BELOW: The Hong Kong apartment living
room of interior designer Louise Kou features
a confident mixture of traditional collectibles
and contemporary furniture.

SPACEDININGROOMS

ABOVE: A rough-hewn plank from an old tree supported simply on a trestle arrangement.

LEFT: In a country club north of Beijing, a table and chairs that follow traditional designs but are compressed for low-level sitting and dining.

ABOVE: In a small cubic house designed by Makoto Koizumi, with a floor plan of only 320 square feet, the space is multi-purpose. The dining area looks out onto a stone platform that functions as a veranda.

RIGHT: A simple, solid dining table in a dining space fashioned underneath a suspended staircase in a villa near Delhi, India.

RIGHT: An austere Japanese-style dining room with a low cherrywood table and walls covered in handmade paper. The cushions are also paper-covered.

BELOW: Interior courtyards are a distinctive feature of this house, and the large space between two of the curving glass walls functions as living and dining area for the family.

RIGHT: A kitchen dining area for family meals in a modern villa in Pudong, near Shanghai.

BELOW RIGHT: Using a simple table construction, the dining area in this small apartment is attached to the main living area and lit by a bank of overhead spots.

BELOW: A free-standing sink unit is fitted with a glass top to act as an informal surface for kitchen dining.

TOP LEFT: The formal dining area in the villa featured on the previous page, with serving hatch to the kitchen.

LEFT: An intimate dining space cleverly brought to life by the introduction of a plant, set against the white, brown, and grey of the kitchen furniture.

ABOVE: A sandblasted glass dining table with views through to the swimming pool.

ABOVE: This tutti-frutti terrazzo surface is a surprising but effective combination with the glass-topped dining table and stone floor.

TOP RIGHT: Polished stone floors, white laminate surfaces, and grey velvet-covered chairs make for the ultimate ultra-chic dining experience.

RIGHT: The dining room of a house by Japanese architect Shigeru Ban, overlooking a section of the Great Wall, north of Beijing.

LEFT AND BELOW: Two dining tables by Beijing artist Shao Fan, one (below) in his own house, the other (left) in his neighbour's, feature the artist's hallmark technique of juxtaposing ancient and modern in the same piece.

PAGE LEFT:

TOP: Brick, wood, and concrete combine in this warehouse conversion. A pinewood table and stacking chairs fit perfectly into the setting.

LEFT: In the converted apartment of architect Deng Kun Yan, originally a reception room in an early 20th-century consulate, a long, wood-topped metal table dominates the room, serving as dining table and desk.

RIGHT: A large dining table created in situ by the respected designer Shiro Kuramata. The triple laminate of glass was installed and the centre sheet crazed by being simultaneously cracked with hammers at three points along the edges.

169

ABOVE: A modern Baroque look is achieved using gilding, printed patterns, bright fabrics, glass chandelier and Regency-style chairs.

RIGHT: Dining room by the American-born designer Michael Aram in a New Delhi apartment. A stained wood and metal table and benches add solidity.

TOP LEFT: A Chinese colonial style is created by combining Western decor with Asian touches, such as the hanging scroll and lamp.

TOP RIGHT: Blue-covered high-back armless chairs work well against the gold and muted colours of this interior.

ABOVE: Leather upholstered Victorian dining chairs are a striking contrast with a thin metal table. A Maarten Baas burnt wood sideboard stands out against the white.

LEFT: An expressive table design by Ryoji Suzuki, featuring a glass top on a frame of rough steel and a keel-shaped armature of laminated, carved, and polished wood.

ABOVE: A dark wood modern dining table fits well with a light wood ceiling, white walls, and grey floor.

ABOVE RIGHT: Simple antique-style wooden furniture can be effective if the room itself is composed of varied shapes and textures.

RIGHT: A counter dining area for guests staying in the penthouse apartment of a Shanghai lighting company, designed by architect Kengo Kuma.

SPACESTUDIES

FAR LEFT TOP: Cantilevered steel shelving combined with concealed backlighting help to give a floating quality to the mass of books.

FAR LEFT BOTTOM: Saving space in a small Beijing apartment designed by Zhong Song, a wooden desk backs onto a sofa, with book shelving under the window.

LEFT: A study/living space connected at the right by a corridor to the rest of the house, and featuring a cylindrical console at left that houses kitchen, hi-fi, and television.

BELOW LEFT: A dramatic floor-to-ceiling single-pane glass window makes this study seem like a tree house.

BELOW: For a couple who live and work in an extremely small apartment, this study area saves space by using the underside of storage cupboards to house the desk lighting.

AGE LEFT:
FT: The all-aluminium office of
signer Toshihiko Suzuki, who works
tensively with this material.

GHT TOP: In a minimalist duplex
artment designed by Zhang Zi Hui
d Chen Yi Lang, the small area at the
of the stairs provides an isolated
treat.

GHT BELOW: A study within a large
ring room, with free-standing metal
elving set into an alcove, and a
mber desk.

ABOVE: Part of a rambling tree house
designed by John Gathright, this study is
one of several spaces converted from
giant old Japanese *miso* (fermented
soybean paste) barrels.

RIGHT: A painter's studio close to Beijing
features a large work surface at the
height normally used by calligraphers.

QUIETSPACES

LEFT: Rudolph Schindler's house in West Hollywood, built in 1921–1922, is Japanese-influenced in its minimalism, the plain concrete, with three-inch gaps as windows, giving an air of calm and quiet.

BELOW: JinR, a Beijing designer and restauranteur, designed her own apartment's living area in colours and textures intended to provide a calming atmosphere, using grey and white loose fabrics.

ABOVE: In a Tokyo advertising agency, Klein Dytham Architecture included within the open-plan office area a small space for any employee to retire and think.

ABOVE RIGHT: Designer Toshihiko Suzuki, who specializes in aluminium, created a modern interpretation of a tea-house as a cube of laminated honeycomb aluminium, with circular holes cut for light and ventilation.

RIGHT: Garden designer Toshiya Ogino created this view, towards a slanting maple and rocky slope of ferns, against a curving white wall, for the express purpose of producing a meditative picture when seen from this simple small room.

ABOVE: A hanging balcony known as a *zharooka*, projecting high over the walls of a converted Rajasthani fort, is a tranquil space for meditation or just quietly observing.

LEFT: In an apartment designed by architect Norisada Maeda, a separate area is subtly defined within the living room using a glass wall.

FAR LEFT: In this apartment conversion by architect Deng Kun Yan, a *tatami*-floored space of great simplicity was added as a meditative retreat.

PAGE LEFT: In the Bamboo Wall House, Kengo Kuma adapted the Japanese *engawa*, or projecting verandah, to create a space for contemplation, looking out over the hills near the Great Wall.

ABOVE: A raised bay with *tatami* covering provides space for playing the traditional Japanese game of *go*, in a single-storey dwelling in Kyoto that can be opened or sectioned off with dividers that retreat into the walls.

RIGHT TOP: A substantial private karaoke room in the basement of a large family house in Bangkok, opening onto a below-grade courtyard garden.

RIGHT: Home theatre with projector and low sofa seating in the same house as above.

SPACEPLAY

PAGE LEFT:

CLOCKWISE FROM TOP LEFT: A copper clad wall in the centre of an apartment conversion in which rooms were removed for more entertainment space is both a striking central feature of the room and the surround for the television.

Seen from across the kitchen sink the sitting area of a small, vertically arranged house designed by architect Kohei Sato.

In a house designed by noted architect Yasuo Kondo, the entertainment/sitting area is separated from the dining/kitchen area by a six-feet wide wall.

LEFT: The music room of a Beijing apartment, with dark walls and slate floor, subdued lighting and richly coloured drapes over the window.

LEFT BELOW: The sitting area, which fits into one curved corner, features fitted semi-circular seating built of curved, leather-covered tube-like cushions. The central sections roll out as stools and foot-rests. Above, bunched canvas drapes filter and diffuse the ceiling lights.

BELOW: The key feature here is a large moulded and lacquered unit containing embedded seating and concealed lighting that give a soft, diffused glow. Designed by Rajiv Saini.

SPACELIGHTING

ABOVE: "Kaze" (meaning wind in Japanese), freestanding lights designed by Masayuki Kurokawa, created by wrapping and zipping two oval polypropylene sheets around a lamp.

CLOCKWISE FROM TOP LEFT: In his apartment conversion in the former Japanese consulate, Shanghai, architect Deng Kun Yan, the principal feature in the living-work area, hanging over the long central table, is a light created by folding copper mesh into the form of a giant cloud.
In this double-height living room, natural light from full-height windows shaded by an aluminium grille is supplemented by two circular chandeliers constructed of hundreds of twisted strips of plastic.

"Kanda Nest", a miniature "earth house" built into the top floor of a downtown Tokyo office block. Designed by architect owner Mirai Tono, the curved walls are of mud and straw shaped over steel netting into organic forms. The earthen shell allows space for concealed ceiling lighting to soften the lighting.
[left and right] Akari light sculptures, in mulberry paper and bamboo strips, by Isamu Noguchi, hanging in the self-built granite house of his close friend and collaborator, Masatoshi Izumi.

PREVIOUS PAGES: A sliding screen opens in this *tatami* room to give a low, precisely-framed view of a miniature garden with an island of moss sitting in a sea of white gravel, designed by garden designer Toshiya Ogino. A single concealed spot throws a precisely attenuated beam onto a white wall, creating an illusion of depth by mimicking a sky with the sun just below the horizon.

ABOVE: Miniature halogen capsule lamps at the ends of twisted copper tubing make a sculpture that illuminates this corridor.

ABOVE RIGHT: Backlit acrylic panels set into a low wall and entrance, designed by Atsushi Kitagawara.

FAR RIGHT: A mass of white-painted branches suspended from the ceiling is interwoven with miniature halogen capsule lamps, in a contemporary Beijing tea house.

RIGHT: In this contemporary *tatami* room, with earth plaster walls and wooden ceiling, a thin vertical gap aligned with the edging between two *tatami* mats allows daylight to enter and becomes a design element in its own right.

ABOVE: In a mezzanine sleeping area, concealed strip-lighting under the long shelf near the head of the bed is reflected in the white-painted walls and sloping ceiling for a suffused glow.

LEFT: In this bedroom a Flos floor standing lamp provides a spherical punctuation above a very low window in an otherwise cubic space.

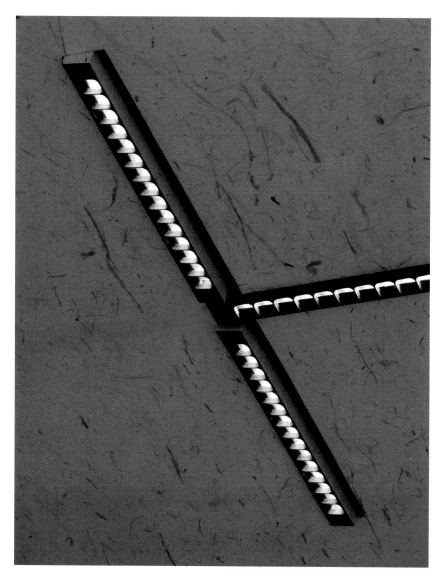

ABOVE: Fibre-optic strips in the ceiling cast a precise pool of light with very little off-axis glare. Lighting designer Shozo Toyohisa.

ABOVE RIGHT: A glass walkway under which is a bed of crushed quartz bordered with miniature halogen capsule lamps.

RIGHT: Wall clad in diagonally laid timber and embedded with lights facing an apartment entrance.

PAGE RIGHT CLOCKWISE FROM TOP LEFT:
A backlit onyx-fronted counter with, behind, shelving on a bare brick wall carrying candles in frosted glass cups.
Lighting unit constructed from an array of industrial caged lamps.
Berry-like symmetrical groupings of light in this hallway.
Clear candle bulbs are used decoratively showing off the glowing element.

TOP: A small rooftop garden installation by Takeshi Nagasaki, in which the concrete and gravel floor is set with two varieties of "stepping stone", one a light in cast glass, the other a disc of copper, each bearing the impression of a section of bamboo.

ABOVE: A trough surrounding a bath is base-lit with lamps that cycle in colour, shining through a bed of pebbles.

TOP RIGHT: Glass cube light designed by Takeshi Nagasaki, made by blowing into a form containing the rough surfaces of the actual granite blocks into which the light is finally installed.

RIGHT: A different version of the cube light featured above, in which a few of the surrounding white pebbles were placed in the form before hand-blowing the glass.

ABOVE: Light fitting made from an upturned glass storage jar containing a CFL.

TOP LEFT: Globe lamp designed by architect Terunobu Fujimori, suspended in a net held in a forked branch.

LEFT: A low-voltage halogen spot sited above a square opening cut into a false ceiling of thin bamboo poles lashed together.

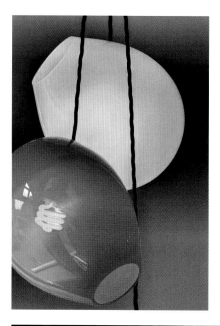
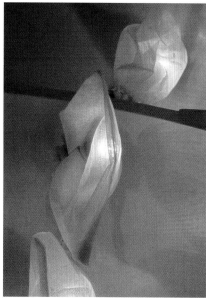

ABOVE FROM LEFT: Hanging from a twisted flex these hand-blown glass lights designed by Jenny Beardshall are based on the shape of a party balloon.
A string of small lights designed by Tsé & Tsé.
A chandelier designed by Piet Boon using molten black polyurethane.
A grey floor light designed by Susanne Phillipson for Pallucco Italia illuminates when the flap is opened.

LEFT: Shigeru Uchida designed this "egg" floor lamp for his tea-room. Two spotlights then highlight the scroll painting and flower.

FOLLOWING PAGES:
LEFT: An all-metal staircase and stairwell, lit deliberately dimly with concealed strip-lighting, to prepare visitors for the subdued illumination on the upper floors.

RIGHT: At the entrance to an innovative Beijing restaurant, the heavy metal door is dramatically lit with a focusing spot at a raking angle, while the secret opening mechanism is a sensor in the base-lit urn, which reacts to a hand passing over it.

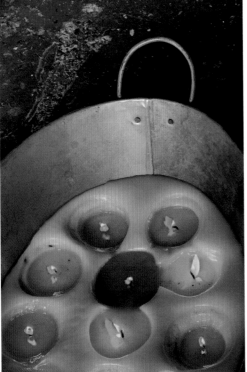

ABOVE LEFT: A sense of playfulness is continued in this living room by the "bulb-bird" ceiling light.

ABOVE: A helicopter light hovers above this counter.

LEFT: A multi-wicked candle has been made inside this tin pail.

SPACEMEZZANINES

LEFT: For a private retreat in a double-height open-plan family house, Norisada Maeda suspended this small study like a perch in one high corner.

RIGHT: Elegantly integrating storage and sleeping spaces, a mezzanine bedroom was cleverly created above walk-in cupboards.

LEFT: A large wooden platform serves as a enclosed bedroom – an internal tree house It sits beneath a barn-like roof.

RIGHT: A small cube-proportioned house finished, all in wood, makes the most of the space by fitting a mezzanine instead of a fully closed-off floor.

BELOW: In a conversion of a 1930s' apartment, a simple and open mezzanine at one end of the living space serves as study and small sitting area, remaining connected with the rest of the apartment.

ABOVE: In a house designed partly as a private gallery, an upper floor connecting walkway with sandblasted glass panels doubles as a viewing platform.

LEFT: All-wood construction with a natural finish. Translucent polycarbonate sheets on diagonal trusses cover the façade and add a measure of privacy.

SPACEBALCONIES

TOP: In this strikingly modern structure architect Shigeharu Isaka, steel balconies and walkways obviate the need for an upper floor.

ABOVE: The Hardy residence in Bali was modelled after an Iban longhouse, raised high on timber pillars. A connecting walkway also functions as a sitting out area overlooking the rice terraces.

ABOVE RIGHT: Within the courtyard of this house designed by Jun Tamaki, a tubular steel truss supports a perimeter steel balcony.

RIGHT: For a Tokyo apartment in which the balcony was too small for practical use, artist and garden designer Takeshi Nagasaki created instead a garden installation purely for viewing.

SPACECOURTYARDS

ABOVE: Architect Norisada Maeda designed this house with six internal courtyards, each with glass walls to allow maximum interpenetration of interior and exterior.

LEFT: Designed by the same architect as the house above, this small single-storey dwelling contains a glass dividing wall that completely encloses a narrow courtyard garden exposed to the sky.

FAR LEFT: For this Tokyo house, architects Kazuyo Sejima and Ryue Nishizawa of SANAA excavated part of the plot to create a sunken courtyard, arranged minimally between the two glass-and-polycarbonate walled halves of the residence, with a single dogwood.

FAR LEFT: A centrally planted maple tree is the focus for this entrance courtyard, with a glass wall separating it from the stairway to the main living areas.

LEFT: A sparse and controlled arrangement of two pines set in raked sand, with a wooden deck fringed with Japanese *pachysandra*.

BELOW: High black walls provide privacy for this courtyard planted with grass, maple and *enkianthus*, while granite stepping stones provide a path between two ground-floor rooms.

PAGE LEFT

ABOVE LEFT: A small courtyard with a central arrangement of moss mounds set in white gravel and a single maple, screened from the street by a row of black bamboo.

ABOVE RIGHT: A sloping court paved with rough stones and selective plantings, seen from the plate-glass window at its lower end.

BELOW LEFT: This modern interpretation of a Beijing courtyard house includes several small glass-enclosed courtyards designed for viewing and admitting light.

BELOW RIGHT: A small courtyard planted with a maple set in gravel lies at the bottom of a three-storey light well, viewable from all levels.

SPACEINSIDEOUTSIDE

TOP LEFT: Built on the only available space, over the parking area of her parents' house, architect Yoko Matsumura designed her study/apartment to connect with the mid-levels of two old gingko trees.

TOP RIGHT: In a contemporary Balinese house, glass walls extend the terrace area into an air-conditioned dining room.

BOTTOM: A full-height glass box encloses a miniature courtyard open to the sky.

BELOW: In the study of a house near Pattaya, Thailand, glass panels on an end wall and ceiling, coupled with the long wall of horizontal wooden planking, create continuity between the study and the garden.

PREVIOUS PAGES:
LEFT: Glass sheets bonded without frames give total transparency onto the entrance patio of this lane house converted by architectural practice sciskewcollaborative.

RIGHT TOP: A small roof terrace constructed around a penthouse bathroom.

RIGHT BELOW: Kengo Kuma's Lotus House features a series of walls of thin travertine slabs in an open chequerboard pattern to allow interpenetration.

ABOVE: For a small London house, architect ...n Chee arranged folding glass doors that ...n be fully opened to connect the living ...ace with the small terrace.

...AR LEFT: The Plastic House, Tokyo, by ...engo Kuma, uses both glass and FRP ...rethane slatted walls to open the structure.

...EFT: The projecting living area of this ...eekend villa ends in a picture window that ...ecisely frames the woodland view.

ABOVE: The penthouse suite of a Shanghai building overlooking a garden. Interior and exterior connect by means of an infinity pool interlocked with glass-walled sitting areas.

RIGHT: Small interior courts maintain a sense of openness in a retreat near Mumbai designed by Samira Rathod.

LEFT: A beach house in Hua Hin, Thailand, designed by architectural practice A49, surrounds the main living area with water views of the swimming pool and sea.

ABOVE: Modernism meets the jungle. A Ray Eames lounge chair and Isamu Noguchi paper lamp are set off by the green backdrop including a pond seemingly ready to flood the room.

SPACETERRACES

T: An 11th-floor apartment in Akasaka, o, designed by its owner-architect, Kisho kawa, to contain a secluded garden with ouse.

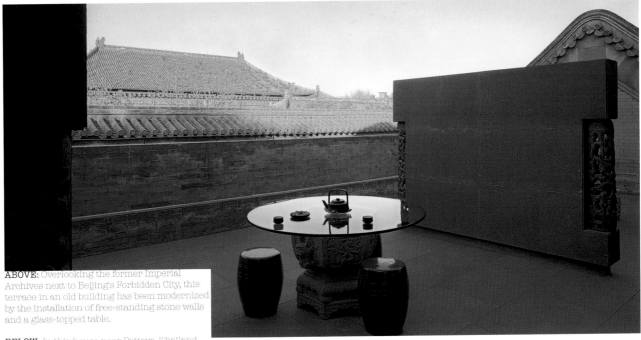

ABOVE: Overlooking the former Imperial Archives next to Beijing's Forbidden City, this terrace in an old building has been modernized by the installation of free-standing stone walls and a glass-topped table.

BELOW: In this house near Pattaya, Thailand, by architects A49, traditional principles of upper-floor terraces shaded by projecting eaves have been reworked in a modern idiom to create a dwelling that remains cool without air conditioning.

FAR LEFT: Near Hua Hin, Thailand, this seaside villa has a small pool on the top floor, the decking shaded from the sub-tropical sun by metal slatting.

LEFT: Access to this roof terrace is protected by a specially built polycarbonate hatch that functions as a skylight.

BELOW: A simple surround of brick wall for this roof terrace is animated by regular perforations to allow light and breeze without sacrificing privacy.

SPACEURBANGARDENS

LEFT: The small garden in Plastic House, Tokyo, by Kengo Kuma, is softened and lightened by the use of FRP (fibreglass-reinforced plastic) for raised platform and walls, with a characteristic milky green appearance.

ABOVE: An enclosed garden-for-viewing with a single silver birch and stone water-basin is sited at the end of the main corridor of the house, sealed by glass on the interior and a metal grille on the exterior.

LEFT: A tiny basement space imaginatively converted into a step-garden by the use of railway sleepers to make descending ledges seasonally planted.

RIGHT TOP: Sculptural simplicity is the theme for this small courtyard garden, achieved with an area of raised decking, a pebble-bordered lawn and white walls, with three young maples to provide the vertical.

RIGHT BELOW: Along the side of an apartment block, the narrow gap is designed to be seen in plan from the balconies above: an arrangement of gravel set with volcanic boulders and stones.

FOLLOWING PAGES:
LEFT:
TOP LEFT: A small roof terrace of green lawn looks out onto a courtyard. Full-length glazing of the three inward-facing sides of house maximize exposure to nature.

RIGHT: A small garden behind glass against the outside wall contains a hand-carved stone water basin, a mound of moss with softened irregular edges set in gravel, and Oriental paperbush.

BELOW: A symbolic garden designed by Takeshi Nagasaki that follows the principle of opposites, divided between light (the overlapping concrete discs) and dark (obscure miniature landscape below them).

RIGHT:
TOP : In a Shanghai studio garden, a moongate built of recycled bricks at left is reflected in an effective illusion by a large mirror wall at right.

BELOW: A raised terrace garden in Primrose Hill, London, with concrete stepping stones set in black soil. The planting is predominantly evergreen, with a *chusan* palm and a border of grasses and ferns.

ABOVE: The garden of a terraced house in Kensington, London, reworked by garden designer Takeshi Nagasaki with multi-layered walls in surfaces that vary from the original 1830s' brickwork to blackened wood burnt with a blowtorch and bamboo. Steel mirrors at left help create an illusory space where sections of stone flagging and wall have been removed.

UTILITY

KITCHENS
BATHROOMS
SHOWER ROOMS
BASINS
TOILETS
BEDROOMS
STORAGE
SHELVING
BOOKSHELVES

Here we have taken a broader-than-usual definition of utility, to include the necessary functions of life, as opposed to the recreational ones. However, as we will see in the pages that follow, even the utilitarian can be approached in a creative and imaginative way. Utility can be enjoyed.

Our perceptions of the kitchen, what it should contain and how it should function, have undergone a fundamental change, because cooking itself has become progressively more integrated in many people's lifestyles. This is not universal, of course, but there is a growing minority who see cooking as the opportunity for creative expression or winding down, rather than as just a necessary chore. This in turn means that more effort and money are spent on furnishing and equipping the kitchen, and more time spent in it, as friends gather during the preparation. And with efficient, industrial-strength extractors, it becomes practical to include a kitchen in an open-plan living and dining area, as we saw in the last chapter.

Bathrooms are another "utility" space that have been elevated in perception, and so attract more expenditure and effort, suggesting that more time is being spent in them. The idea of a bath as an entertaining experience is nothing new to the Japanese, who have taken bathing to an advanced level, even as a form of destination tourism. The bath then becomes a place for soaking and relaxing and not for cleaning (which takes place before and separately). And closely associated, what of toilets, surely the most functional of all units in the home? Some of the examples here may surprise, as their designers have sought to make going to the toilet — well, fun.

Sleeping may be functional, but the space where we do it is also undergoing an overhaul. There are two trends in evidence here. One is towards enlarging and more fully equipping bedrooms as places to house more than just a bed, and where the ambience and view are fully considered. The other is towards minimizing the impact of sleeping on the total space available. One strategy is to build mezzanines and similar extensions within existing space; another is to follow the Japanese tradition of time-sharing between sleeping and living — a futon that can be rolled and stored during the day.

It's interesting for me that even the mundane in interiors, the working necessities of plumbing, storage and so on, are receiving thoughtful design attention. Contemporary interiors are developing and changing faster and in more imaginative ways than ever before. We are, on the whole, less hidebound by our own traditions, more ready to accept ideas from other cultures, more willing to experiment. And all of this is fuelled by changing styles of life and a globalization of ideas and creativity.

UTILITYKITCHENS

ABOVE: A two-tiered counter in Japanese oak and stainless steel zig-zags through the centre of the kitchen finished in ink-stained timber and straw-flecked earthen plaster.

LEFT: In this open-space, double-height house, a curved free-standing wall in the centre shelters the kitchen, in stainless steel, fitted with bulkhead lights and a porthole through to the main room.

ABOVE: In this all-glass house designed by architect Koh Kitayama, one long, narrow box is inserted midway into the main structure of a building which houses living area and utilities. From the central kitchen/dining section of the unit, sliding screens open out onto the remainder of the triple-height space.

RIGHT: The angular lines of the central stainless steel cooking and sink unit with extractor in the small kitchen are softened by partly surrounding it with an oval, granite-topped eating counter.

RIGHT: Open-plan kitchen and dining area with fitted oak cupboard walls and white laminate table on stainless steel plinth. An industrial extractor is necessary as this space adjoins the living area.

BELOW RIGHT: Basement kitchen with a solid oak table, the floor in diagonally-laid old Chinese bricks with walls and ceiling in unpainted concrete.

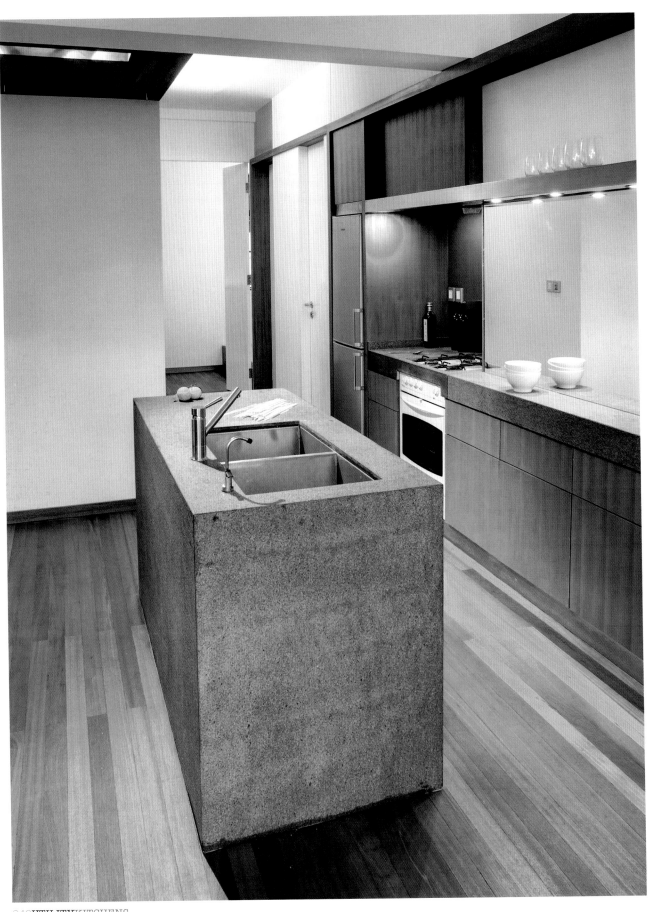

LEFT: A nomadic sink unit made from cast concrete, and echoed in the work surface opposite, stands as an interruption to the refined wood floor and cupboard doors.

ABOVE: This kitchen is separated from a study space by a large pivoting door that, when open, seems to float in the middle of the space.

RIGHT: Within this open plan kitchen/ living/dining space, wood, stone and light earth colours allow for a sophisticated but understated solution.

FAR LEFT: In an open-plan small weekend villa, the kitchen, separated from the remainder of the space by a glass partition, is in the form of a black trench with underfloor cupboards, the work surfaces being at floor level.

LEFT: An imaginative conversion of a 1930s' apartment by architects sciskewcollaborative, in which walnut and plywood units interpenetrate the existing structure, carrying utilities and providing storage, here surrounding the kitchen area.

BELOW: A kitchen conversion in which white laminate surfaces contrast with a ceiling on which timber and mosaic intersect.

RIGHT: At one end of a combined living/dining area in a conversion in London by Ian Chee, the kitchen worktop, sink and cooking unit are neatly contained in a recess in the far wall of the living/dining area. Concealed strip-lighting supplements the generous skylight.

BELOW: A fixed high table and three bar stools offer a clever solution for eating in a small kitchen space.

BELOW RIGHT: Black glass with stainless steel edging for the kitchen units echoes Art Deco style in this modern apartment conversion.

RIGHT TOP: A cool atmosphere is created by combining bleached wood floors, white kitchen units, black stools, and kitchen work surface.

RIGHT: Here exposed grey brick walls and stone floor have been used to add contrast to the smooth white kitchen.

FAR RIGHT: An open-plan live/work area with study, dining room, and kitchen all in one. A subtle white partition helps divide up the space without boxing the rooms in.

UTILITYBATHROOMS

ABOVE: Water pours in from the wall at left and exits into a sunken trough at floor level, turning a basin into a water feature.

LEFT: Finished with a rough cement render, a wave-like interior wall turns a very ordinary apartment layout into something special. Streaks of iridescent mosaic enliven it further. The bathtub is handbuilt from stone.

FAR LEFT: Designed by Beijing artist Shao Fan for the house of a friend and neighbour, the circular theme continues through from room to skylight to bathtub. Even the shelf and storage, in grey brick, are designed as a quadrant that intersects with the plinth.

LEFT: Restricted space in this house is utilized simply by sectioning off the bathroom with two glass panels, and cutting a triangular window.

RIGHT: Titled "Phytolab" by its creator, French designer Matali Crasset, this bathroom is enclosed with 100 plant pots set in acrylic panels.

ABOVE: An outsized porthole for this Japanese-style bathroom near Tokyo gives a view over a sheltered garden.

RIGHT: An angled full-length skylight floods this bathroom with light. The basins are partly set into a marble counter.

LEFT: Japanese architect Kengo Kuma created this bathroom in a penthouse suite at the top of a Shanghai office building for visiting clients. The slatted wooden floor is mirrored in the electrically-operated ceiling, with louvres that open and close.

BELOW: A bathroom with a view, high in a modernized Rajasthani fort overlooking the Aravali Hills. Bathtub, floor, and walls are in marble.

RIGHT: An old free-standing tub in a Raj-themed bathroom conversion designed by Mirjana Oberoi.

FAR RIGHT: Hand-painted cloth over Indian chick bamboo screens create an outdoor bathroom on the penthouse terrace of an old building in Delhi.

BELOW RIGHT: A spa bathroom in Jaipur, built around an existing mature neem tree (*Azadirachta indica*), known for its medicinal qualities.

ABOVE: A Japanese-style *ofuro*, combining sunken hot tub and wall shower for washing before bathing, but unusually set next to a traditional *tatami* room.

LEFT: A sunken marble bath with a sloping backrest, with views of a small walled garden

FAR LEFT: A restricted space for the bathroom, but the view is extended with sliding windows onto an alcove set with fern-and-moss-covered rocks and a bamboo screen.

LEFT: The sinuous curves of the bath tub and wall, covered in white mosaic, soften the stark minimal white treatment of this bathroom.

BELOW: All the daylight entering this house is through deep light wells, which allows complete privacy and, for the bathroom, open glass walls.

LEFT: Distorted in this wide-angle view, a bathroom conversion in a Victorian house in London features diffused and backlit sandblasted glass panels to enclose an old iron bathtub and storage space.

BELOW LEFT: A restored Art Deco bathroom featuring tiles by the British company Original Style, and a reproduction Tamara de Lempicka painting.

BELOW: Two examples of the all-white marble bath. In the lower example a built-in marble backrest and "pillow" are included.

RIGHT: The unusual angles in this bathroom conversion inspired the architect-designers to create interlocking patterns of surface finishes – polished concrete and tiles – extending this treatment to the ceiling.

BELOW RIGHT: Palms and other trees screen the floor-to-ceiling window of this light, airy bathroom in a seaside villa south of Bangkok.

ABOVE: This bath is set into the concrete foundations of a modern villa. All partitions are glass, the one behind the bathtub is a one-way mirror to conceal the toilet.

TOP RIGHT: An organically shaped bathtub in concrete mixed with beach pebbles, which continues into the floor.

RIGHT: An egg-shaped bathroom peppered with small portholes in the landmark 1994 Japanese dwelling titled the Soft and Hairy House, by Uchida Findlay Partnership. The interior wall surface is covered in small circular rubberized tiles.

RIGHT: A striking angled plate-glass bathroom designed by Norisada Maeda occupies centre stage in this residence, surrounded by kitchen, dining and living areas.

UTILITYSHOWERROOMS

RIGHT: A trough filled with white pebbles for drainage in a roof-terrace shower.

LEFT: A shower featuring a Bisazza glass mosaic.

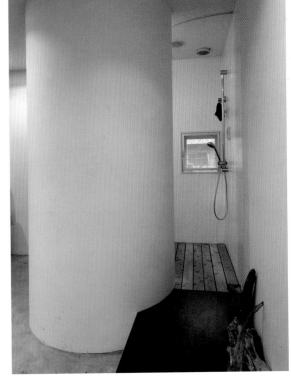

ABOVE: In the centre of the unusual bathroom featured on page 258, a central unit houses toilet, shower, Japanese-style low taps, and urinal.

ABOVE RIGHT: A tiny exterior garden adjacent to the shower/bathroom.

LEFT: In a small Tokyo apartment, a shower partitioned by plastic curtains, with all fittings made from plumbing pipes.

RIGHT: A shower tucked away behind a circular unit containing the toilet.

RIGHT: A glass wall onto the bedroom integrates this minimalist shower.

MIDDLE: Architect Rajiv Saini gave a tent-like character to this shower and bathroom by adding a spotlit hand-painted textile ceiling.

FAR RIGHT: A stone and timber shower unit built for a large tent in a Rajasthani encampment.

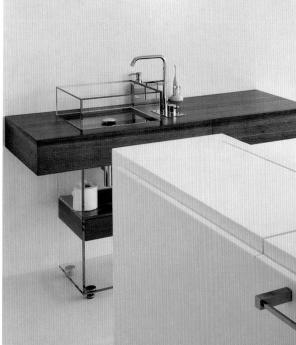

UTILITYBASINS

FAR LEFT: A dished glass bowl makes the simplest possible washbasin.

LEFT TOP: A rectangular washbasin in glass is continued below the wooden shelf for storage, forming two intersecting structures.

LEFT BELOW: The view of the grey marble walls and floor is left uninterrupted by the use of glass and steel in this striking bathroom.

THIS PAGE: A pervading marine theme for this seaside bungalow by Aniket Bhagwat is continued in a washing area separated from the dining area by a freestanding partition, in the form of a stainless steel "wave".

ABOVE: In a Singapore house, a single thick slab of dark granite is left roughly chipped at the edges, but hollowed out with a smooth sloping curve.

MIDDLE TOP: A simple ceramic bowl basin in an understated earth-coloured setting.

MIDDLE RIGHT: A ceramic dished bowl in designer Ken Jenkins' own home.

RIGHT TOP: Raw plaster wall combines with a marble surface and bowl in this simple small basin unit.

RIGHT: A blue glass inverted cone hangs from a glass top, with drainage at the apex.

ABOVE: A large oval basin by Catalano was chosen for its resemblance to traditional Chinese stone basins by designer Peter Aiken, who also custom-made the simply turned stainless steel towel rails.

RIGHT TOP: A generously proportioned Victorian washstand fits comfortably into a modernized bathroom with large rectangular tiles and sandblasted backlit glass cupboards.

RIGHT: A white ceramic bowl sits lightly on a dark polished granite slab surrounded by wood and raw plaster walls.

FAR LEFT: A copper stand washbasin supported by spiral ironwork designed by Linda Garland in her Bali home.

LEFT: Brass, a common material for utensil in India, is here put to use as a washbasin i country home.

BELOW LEFT: A wood basin set into an all-bamboo washroom designed by Kengo Kur.

BOTTOM LEFT: Bamboo, thatch, and adobe are the key materials in the Green School opened by John Hardy in Bali. One of the class washrooms.

BELOW: In John Hardy's own Bali home, a washbasin in polished brass, with locally carved wooden tap handles.

FAR RIGHT: Many Tokyo house plots are irregularly shaped, and for this wedge-shap plot the difficult apex has been successfully converted into a small washroom.

RIGHT: Ceramic artist Yuichi Kurosawa use one of his own creations as a washbasin, wi an unobtrusive central drainage hole.

BELOW RIGHT: Twin freestanding washbasins in stone.

UTILITYTOILETS

LEFT: The ladies' toilet at the top of the Hotel Torni, Helsinki, is widely regarded as having one of the best views of the city.

ABOVE: In a seaside property in Thailand, the toilet, set within the bathroom, is given a fine view across the pebble-filled ledge towards the sea.

ABOVE: Bathroom and toilet featuring stainless steel and white walls, showing how simple decorative black and white tiles can be used to dramatic effect.

ABOVE RIGHT: On the lower level of this Ba villa, with privacy afforded by the terrace overhang and by its steep hillside location, t toilet adjoining a bedroom looks out over th valley below.

RIGHT: This bedroom in a contemporary vi in Seminyak, Bali, opens onto a courtyard bathroom and toilet, designed by architect I Chee.

FOLLOWING PAGE:

TOP LEFT: A small circular toilet, separate from the main house, has an an earthen wall supported by undressed small tree trunks, wood planking ceiling, and a floor of stones set in concrete.

TOP RIGHT: In a corner of the Linda Garland House, Bali, a toilet is set under the low bamboo eaves, protected by a simple white net curtain.

BOTTOM LEFT: The toilet in a Jaipur farmhouse converted by Munnu Kasliwal is finished in a dragged terracotta wash, with simple brass fittings.

BOTTOM RIGHT: The toilet and shower of a luxury tent, originally designed for the Maharajah of Jodhpur, set on a concrete footing.

275

ABOVE AND RIGHT: A family toilet in the woods near Helsinki, Finland, for a weekend villa. The simple rustic design is for a couple and small child to share.

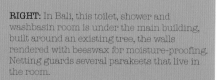

RIGHT: In Bali, this toilet, shower and washbasin room is under the main building, built around an existing tree, the walls rendered with beeswax for moisture-proofing. Netting guards several parakeets that live in the room.

FAR RIGHT: In the Green School, Bali, sound ecological principles rule. The twin toilets are divided for solid and liquid matter.

UTILITYBEDROOMS

PREVIOUS PAGE: On the top floor of this beachfront villa in Hua Hin, Thailand, full-height glass walls on three sides of the master bedroom give a panoramic view of the seaside location.

FAR LEFT: The bedroom in a penthouse apartment, with a wooden plinth for the bed, has an electrically-operated louvred ceiling to control the daylight.

LEFT: A bedroom in a property with extensive grounds near Delhi, designed by Rajiv Saini. The picture window exploits the view to the maximum.

BELOW: A bedroom in Shigeru Ban's Furniture House looking out over hills north of Beijing. The walls are the architect's invention, a lightweight but structural laminate of woven bamboo strips.

ABOVE: This ground-floor bedroom in a small London house conversion receives ample diffuse light through two sections of sandblasted glass - one the window onto the mews, the other sealing the staircase.

TOP RIGHT: To maximize the use of limited space in this top-floor apartment, one bedroom is extended under the eaves, with a skylight added, to give just enough room for a futon.

FAR RIGHT: A u-shaped wood-strip platform seems to be hovering above the floor. Ambient downlighting underneath the bed exaggerates this effect in this very narrow apartment.

RIGHT: Bedroom in the apartment of architect Shigeru Ban. The hinged panels at far right conform to the curved ceiling and can be closed seamlessly. The lounger is a Ban design, made of cardboard tubing.

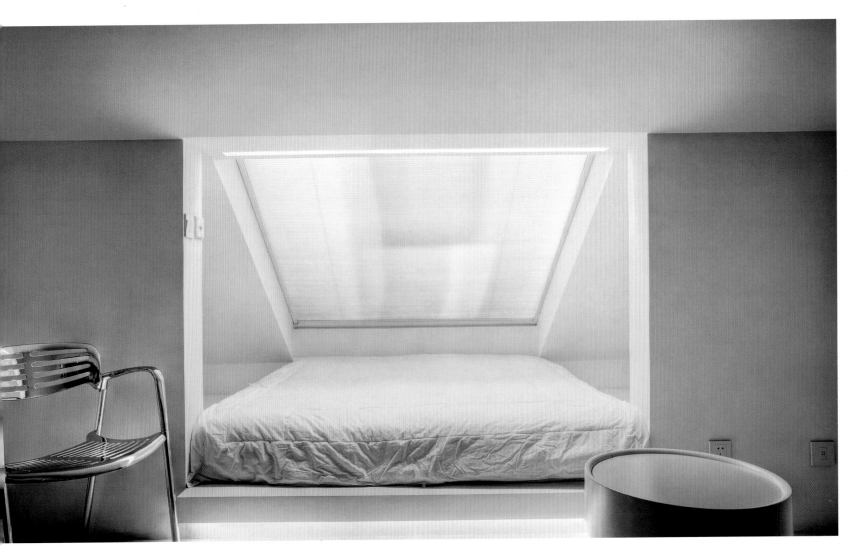

TOP LEFT: This all-white bedroom with polished tile floor is treated in a minimalist Japanese fashion, with the futon packed away in the cupboards during the day.

LEFT: A simple, almost austere bedroom, with futon and tatami mats in a plain white room, in the Bamboo Wall House designed by Kengo Kuma. The bamboo poles outside are a part of the building's façade.

ABOVE: In this apartment conversion, also featured on page 243, architects sciskewcollaborative used computer modelling to plan the multi-faceted wooden units that interpenetrate the existing rooms, carrying utilities, providing storage space, and containing the bed.

TOP: A contemporary four-poster bed in stained oak, designed as a minimally cubic frame.

ABOVE: Cream-coloured curtains diffuse the light for a warm glow throughout this bedroom by Dutch interior designer Natasja van der Meer.

RIGHT: Bedroom looking out over a Balinese valley, with bed plinth, floor and wall in continuous sculpted and polished concrete.

ABOVE: In the Vadanyakul House, Bangkok, built by the owner architect, Khun Prabhakorn Vadanyakul of A49 in the middle of a forested plot, glass walls on three sides of the master bedroom bring the forest in, yet the trees themselves ensure privacy.

RIGHT: The open sleeping/bathroom area under the exposed bamboo-and-thatch eaves of Linda Garland's house near Ubud, Bali, with a Chinese four-poster bed.

FAR RIGHT: In the John Hardy House, near Ubud, Bali, the bed is made of recycled ironwood and teak, with mosquito netting made of material normally used for straining tofu.

ABOVE LEFT: Garlands of marigolds, used
throughout India for celebrations and rituals,
add colour and energy to an otherwise
austere white bedroom, in a converted
Rajasthani fort, Devigarh.

BELOW LEFT: A second bedroom in the Hua
Hin house featured on pages 278-279 has
views in both directions along the axis of the
long plot.

LEFT ABOVE: A vibrant mix of strong colours
articulates the space of this Indian bedroom
designed by German owner Jorg Drechsel.
Lathe-turned wooden supports carry the
simple bed, and the wooden wall-panel above
the bed is from an antique chariot.

LEFT BELOW: Bedroom with white marble
plinth and gold leaf floral stencil on the side
wall.

ABOVE: In this bedroom, also in Devigarh,
the recessed headwall is decorated in
traditional *thekri* work – molten glass is
blown into spheres, which are then coated
inside with mercury and broken into pillow-
shaped mirror sections.

RIGHT: A third bedroom in Devigarh
decorated with a lotus theme.

PREVIOUS PAGES:
PAGE LEFT:

TOP: Another bedroom at Devigarh. Each bedroom has a decorative theme; this one features repoussé silver panels covering the headwall.

BOTTOM LEFT: Indian architect Rajiv Saini's bedroom in his own apartment in Mumbai. The intention here is for a crisp, clean, and modern effect.

BOTTOM RIGHT: Wooden bed in Balinese house with mosquito curtains.

PAGE RIGHT:

TOP: Bedroom designed by Kenneth Grant Jenkins, featuring a panel of polished brass sheets in the recess at the head of the bed, exuberant fabrics, and a sofa enclosed in an extension of the wooden platform at the foot.

LEFT: An antique chest from Portuguese Goa with cross and brass candelabra furnish this bedroom by designer/owner Michael Aram, with a floral Indian curtain hung above the head of the bed.

RIGHT: Bedroom designed by Zhong Yaling in a Chinese theme with specifically designed bedspread throw and two red silk lamps that flank the gold lacquer, four-section screen with black ink bamboo drawings at the head of the bed.

LEFT: Bedroom of the Sea Ranch Condominium, California, designed by MLTW American architect Charles Moore in 1964, in the form of a mezzanine platform raised on posts within the central living area, with a four-square canvas hood hanging from the skylight.

RIGHT: A simple bedroom under black ink-stained exposed-timber eaves, contains a futon against a paper-clad wall, with two Akari paper lamps.

UTILITYSTORAGE

LEFT: An ingenious storage and access solution is a sliding steel staircase on tracks set in floor and ceiling. It gives access to an upper storage area, while the cupboard space, into which it fits when not in use, has triangular doors cut to accommodate it.

FAR LEFT: The staircase in a low-cost house in which architect Kazuhiko Namba makes extensive use of plywood is a modern interpretation of the traditional Japanese step-*dansu*, or box steps.

ABOVE: Stainless steel bookstand by Bruno Rainaldi.

TOP: Kitchen shelving arranged perpendicular to the wall in which it is fitted. The three units each slide out fully.

ABOVE: By making the two cupboard doors identical to the door leading from the hall to the living room of this house in Primrose Hill, London, the storage space is effectively concealed.

LEFT TOP: A floor hatch in toughened smoked glass set in a metal frame makes a design feature of access to the cellar.

LEFT BELOW: Steps leading to an attic are concealed behind sliding, white-painted, wooden doors.

BELOW: In contrast to the glass hatch opposite, which draws attention to itself, these hatches leading to a lower storage area appear part of the wooden floor.

TOP RIGHT: Screen-printed cupboard doors by British designer Deborah Bowness.

ABOVE RIGHT: Full-height sliding wooden panels conceal storage units ranged along one wall.

RIGHT: Storage in this contemporary version of a traditional Japanese *tatami* room is in a corner unit suspended from the ceiling.

LEFT AND ABOVE: Storage for books concealed in the steps leading up to a bedroom.

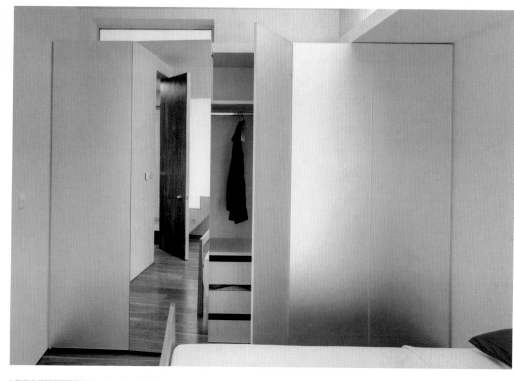

ABOVE: Triangular faceted cupboards in walnut and cherrywood, fitted to the walls of this apartment.

ABOVE RIGHT: Brushed aluminium panels add light and an impression of more space in the constricted confines of this London bedroom.

RIGHT: Sandblasted glass sliding wardrobe doors diffuse the interior lights.

UTILITY SHELVING

PREVIOUS PAGES
LEFT: The sitting area of this living room is
on a raised wooden platform that provides
additional storage space, with a grid of
wooden shelving covering one wall.

RIGHT: An imaginative and simple wine rack
by interior designers Zhang Zi Hui and Chen
Yi Lang, in which the bottles fit sideways.

LEFT: In the library of the China Blue Gallery,
Beijing, with its striking hallway of computer-
cut sculpted panels, the books are housed in a
grid of square, white-painted wooden shelving.

ABOVE: Marble slabs set in a wall provide
shelving to display stone jars.

ABOVE LEFT: A connecting door in a 1905
building, no longer used since its conversion
into separate apartments, has been
transformed into a cupboard by inserting
plain wood shelves.

UTILITYBOOKSHELVES

FAR LEFT: A playful design by Pearl Lam, owner of Contrasts Gallery, for a sitting room in her Shanghai gallery.

LEFT: Using local fitters to build it on site, Peter Oetken devised a narrow steel-frame bookcase that rises through two floors, serving also as one side to the staircase.

LEFT ABOVE: The square box-like sections of this full-height bookcase give extra formality to a study.

FAR LEFT: In this very small apartment, the owners preferred to conceal the book shelving behind white cupboard doors for a visually cleaner effect.

LEFT: For her studio, architect Yoko Matsumura fitted one entire wall with wooden shelving that includes an air-conditioning unit. A folding ladder provides access to the upper shelves.

ABOVE: In a house conversion in Primrose Hill, London, where for one studio-bedroom a mezzanine was constructed under the eaves, the bookcase was fitted all the way to the ceiling, the upper shelves accessible from the meazzanine balcony.

LEFT: To maximize shelf space, this specially designed bookcase was fitted into the steps of an existing staircase.

BELOW: When the clients of architect Jun Tamaki moved to the new house for retirement, they chose to leave their library behind, except one favourite book as a reminder. The architect set it into the living room wall, a recessed shelf for just this volume.

RIGHT: Industrial scaffolding can be ordered in smaller sizes, and in different finishes. A cream-coloured enamel finish was chosen for this construction, which was first planned on paper.

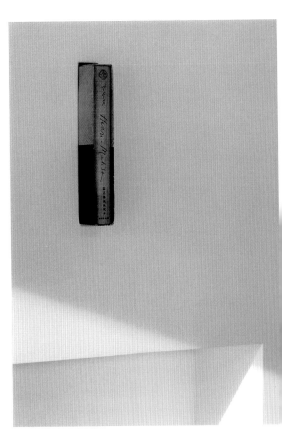

ARCHITECTS/DESIGNERS

A49
Bangkok, Thailand
www.a49.com/en/index.html

A.L.X. (Architect Label Xain)
Tokyo, Japan
www.xain.jp/index.html

Aram, Michael
New York, United States
www.michaelaram.com

Baas, Maarten [Baas & den Herder BV]
Eindhoven-Waalre, the Netherlands
www.maartenbaas.com

Ban, Shigeru [Shigeru Ban Architects]
Tokyo, Japan
www.shigerubanarchitects.com

Bhagwat, Aniket [M/s. Prabhakar B. Bhagwat]
Ahmedabad, India
www.landscapeindia.net

Chee, Ian [VX Design & Architecture]
London, United Kingdom
www.vxdesign.com

Crasset, Matali
Paris, France
www.matalicrasset.com

De Bretteville, Peter [Peter de Bretteville, Architect]
New Haven, United States
www.pdebarc.com

Deng Kun Yan Associates
Shanghai, China

Drechsel, Joerg
Kerala, India
www.malabarhouse.com

Fujimori, Terunobu
Tokyo, Japan
tampopo-house.iis.u-tokyo.ac.jp

Garland, Linda
Bali, Indonesia
www.lindagarland.com

Hardy, John
Bali, Indonesia
www.johnhardy.com

Hui, Zhang Zi
China
northlandstudio@yahoo.com.cn

Ikuyama, Masahide [Arte Spatial Design Studio]
Osaka, Japan
www.arte-sds.jp

Ishida, Toshiaki [Toshiaki Ishida Architect & Associates]
Tokyo, Japan
homepage2.nifty.com/ishida-archi/index.html

Izue, Kan [Kan Izumi Architect & Associates]
Osaka, Japan
www.izue.co.jp

Izumi, Masatoshi
Kagawa, Japan
www.izumi-stoneworks.com

Jain, Bijoy [Studio Mumbai]
Mumbai, India
www.studiomumbai.com

Jenkins, Kenneth Grant [JK arq]
Shanghai, China
www.jkarq.com

JinR
Beijing, China

JKarQ Architectural Design Firm
Shanghai, China
www.jkarq.com

Kasliwal, Munnu
Jaipur, India
www.gempalacejaipur.com

Kawaguchi, Michimasa
[Michimasa Kawaguchi Architects and Associates]
Tokyo, Japan
www.wako-car.co.jp/michimasa/e/main-e.html

Kihara, Chitoshi [Chitoshi Kihara Architect & Associates]
Osaka, Japan
www.kihara-sekkei.com

Kita, Toshiyuki
Osaka, Japan
www.toshiyukikita.com

Kitagawara, Atsushi [Atsushi Kitagawa Architects]
Tokyo, Japan
www.kitagawara.co.jp

Kitayama, Koh [Architecture Workshop Ltd]
Tokyo, Japan
www.archws.com

Klein Dytham Architecture
Tokyo, Japan
www.klein-dytham.com

Koizumi, Makoto [Koizumi Studio]
Tokyo, Japan
www.koizumi-studio.jp

Kondo, Yasuo [Yasuo Kondo Design]
Tokyo, Japan
www.kon-do.co.jp

Kou. Louise [KOU]
Hong Kong, China
www.kouconcept.com

SELECTED STORES

BERLIN

Design-Store	Helmholtzstraße 2–9, 10625 Berlin Charlottenburg www.design-store.de	49 (0)30 3152484 mail@design-store.de
Kollwitz 45	Kollwitzstr. 45, 10405 Berlin Prenzlauer Berg www.kollwitz45.de	49 (0)30 44010413 info@kollwitz45.de
Odama	Steinstraße 37, 10119 Berlin Mitte www.odama.de	49 (0)30 23455785 welcome@odama.de
Puri Design	Rosa-Luxemburg-Straße 5, 10178 Berlin www.puridesign.com	49 (0)30 25762273
Schönhauser Design-Möbel + Objekte	Neue Schönhauser Straße 18, 10178 Berlin Mitte www.schoenhauser-design.de	49 (0)30 2811704 mail@schoenhauser-design.de
Schönhauser Design	Weinmeisterstraße 12, 10178 Berlin	49 (0)30 32669159
Schönhauser Räume	Kastanienallée 55, 10119 Berlin Mitte	49 (0)30 48625606
stilwerk	Kantstraße 17, 10623 Berlin www.stilwerk.de	49 (0)30 315150 berlin@stilwerk.de
wohnzone – berlin	Eberstraße 33, 10827 Berlin Schöneberg www.wohnzone-berlin.de	49 (0)30 3152096 wohnzone-berlin@web.de

LONDON

Aram	110 Drury Lane, Covent Garden, London WC2B 5SG www.aram.co.uk	44 (0)20 7557 7557 aramstore@aram.co.uk
Conran Shop	Michelin House, 81 Fulham Road, London SW3 6RD www.conran.com	44 (0)20 7589 7401 fulham@conran.com
Coexistence	288 Upper Street, London N1 2TZ www.coexistence.co.uk	44 (0)20 7354 8817 enquiries@coexistence.co.uk
London Lighting Company	135 Fulham Road, London SW3 6RT www.londonlighting.co.uk	44 (0)20 7589 3612
Mint	2 North Terrace, London SW3 2BA www.mintshop.co.uk	44 (0)20 7224 4406 info@mintshop.co.uk
SCP	135–139 Curtain Road, London EC2A 3BX www.scp.co.uk	44 (0)20 7739 1869 info@scp.co.uk
twentytwentyone	274 Upper Street, London N1 2UA www.twentytwentyone.com	44 (0)20 7288 1996 shop@twentytwentyone.com
Unto This Last	230 Brick Lane, London E2 7EB www.untothislast.co.uk	44 (0)20 7613 0882 info@UntoThisLast.co.uk
Viaduct	1–10 Summers Street, London EC1R 5BD www.viaduct.co.uk	44 (0)20 7278 8456 info@viaduct.co.uk

MILAN

Danese	Via Canova, 34, 20145 Milano www.danesemilano.com	39 02 34939534 info@danesemilano.com
Dilmos	Piazza S. Marco, 1, 20121 Milano www.dilmos.com	39 02 29002437 info@dilmos.it
Galleria Luisa delle Piane	Via G.Giusti, 24, 20154 Milano	39 02 3319680
High Tech	Piazza XXV Aprile, 12, 20124 Milano www.high-techmilano.com	39 02 62411058 info@cargomilano.it
10 Corso Como	Corso Como, 10, 20124 Milano www.10corsocomo.com	39 02 29002674 shop@10corsocomo.com
De Padova	Corso Venezia, 14, 2021 Milano www.depadova.it	39 02 777201 info@depadova.it
Galleria Post Design	Via della Moscova, 27, 20121 Milano www.memphismilano.it	39 02 6554731 postdesign@tiscali.it
Spazio Tashi Delek	Via Marco Polo, 4, 20124 Milano www.tashidelekmilano.com	39 02 29061806 info@tashidelekmilano.it

PARIS

Boutique Bo	52, rue Sainte-Croix de la Bretonnerie, 75004 Paris	33 (0)1 42 71 68 98
Galerie Downtown	33, rue de Seine, 75006, Paris www.galeriedowntown.com	33 (0)1 46 33 82 41 contact@galeriedowntown.com
Galerie Kreo	31, rue Dauphine, 75006 Paris www.galeriekreo.com	33 (0)1 53 10 23 00 kreogal@wanadoo.fr
Galerie Philippe Jousse	18, rue de Seine, 75006 Paris www.jousse-entreprise.com	33 (0)1 53 82 13 60 infos@jousse-entreprise.com
Galerie Patrick Seguin	5, rue des Taillandiers, 75011 Paris www.patrickseguin.com	33 (0)1 4700 3235 info@patrickseguin.com
Galerie Yves Gastou	12, rue Bonaparte, 75006 Paris www.galerieyvesgastou.com	33 (0)1 53 73 00 10 contact@galerieyvesgastou.com
Mouvements Modernes	112–114 rue la boétie, 75008 Paris www.mouvementsmodernes.com	33 (0)1 45 08 08 82 info@mouvementsmodernes.com

NEW YORK

Aero	419 Broome Street, New York, NY 10013 www.aerostudios.com	1 212 966 1500
BDDW	5 Crosby Street, New York, New York, NY 10013 www.bddw.com	1 212 625 1230 info@bddw.com
Kiosk	95 Spring Street between Broadway and Mercer, 2nd Floor, New York, NY 10012 http://kioskkiosk.com	1 212 226 8601 info@kioskkiosk.com
The Future Perfect	115 North 6th Street, Brooklyn, New York 11211 www.thefutureperfect.com	1 718 599 6278 hello@thefutureperfect.com
Matter	405 Broome Street, New York, NY 10013 www.mattermatters.com	1 212 343 2600 info@mattermatters.com
Michelle Varian	35 Crosby Street, New York, NY 10013 www.michelevarian.com	1 212 343 0033 varianmichele@aol.com
Ochre	462 Broome Street, New York, NY 10013 http://shop.ochrestore.com	1 212 414 4332 orders@ochrestore.com
Ted Muehling	27 Howard Street, NYC 10013 www.tedmuehling.com	1 212 431 3825 tmuehling@gmail.com

BEIJING

Crossover Space	No. 81 Sanlitun bei Jie, Chaoyang District, Beijing	86 10 52086113
Nest	Room 202, building 3, no. 210 Taikang Road, Beijing www.jooi.com	86 21 64736193
Shanghai 100%	No. 71 Wuyuan road, near Wulumuqi Road, Beijing www.100percentshanghai.com	86 21 5404 1678
Zizaoshe	G2 Zhongliang Square, Beijing www.zizaoshe.com	86 10 8511 8611

TOKYO

Actus	BYGS bldg 1F&2F, 2-19-1 Shinjuku, Shinjuku-ku, Tokyo 160-0022 www.actus-interior.com	81 (0)3 3350 6011
Aidec	Aoyama Tower Bldg Annex 1F, 2-24-15 Minami-Aoyama, Minato-ku, Tokyo 107-0062 www.aidec.jp	81 (0)3 5772 6660
The Harlem	1F, 1-28-9 Higashi, Shibuya-ku, Tokyo 150-0011 www.hadeux.com/theharlem/japanese/mainframe.html	81 (0)3 5774 1794 shop@hadeux.co.jp
hhstyle.com Harajuku	6-14-2 Jingumae, Shibuya-ku, Tokyo 150-0001 www.hhstyle.com	81 (0)3 3400 3434
Idee	2-16-29 Jiyugaoka, Meguro-ku, Tokyo 152-0035 www.idee.co.jp	81 (0)3 5701 7555
mYwaY	CODAN CANAL COURT BLOCK3 3A/3B, 1-9-17 Shinonome, Koto-ku, Tokyo 135-0062 www.bytrico.com/index.html	81 (0)3 3532 1901
Tendo Ply	Fukazawa Bldg 2F, 4-35-7 Fukazawa, Setagaya-ku, Tokyo 158-0081 www.tendo-ply.jp	81 (0)3 5758 7111

INDEX

eightbooks

Published in 2009 by
Eight Books Limited
18 Elwin Street
London E2 7BU
t + 44 (0)20 7729 2781
info@8books.co.uk
www.8books.co.uk

A catalogue record for this book is available from the British Library.

ISBN 978 0 9554322 4 8

Printed in China

Also published by Eight Books:
New Zen: The tea-ceremony room in modern Japanese architecture
ISBN: 978 0 9554322 0 0
Street Art Chile
ISBN: 978 0 9554322 1 7
Mute Magazine: Graphic Design
ISBN: 978 0 9554322 2 4
Gumuchdjian Architects: Selected Works
ISBN: 978 0 9554322 3 1